WITHDRAWN

SIR WALTER RALEGH

MEN AND BOOKS

SIR WALTER RALEGH

by

PHILIP EDWARDS

LONGMANS, GREEN AND CO
LONDON ❖ NEW YORK ❖ TORONTO

LONGMANS, GREEN AND CO LTD
6 & 7 CLIFFORD STREET LONDON W I
ALSO AT MELBOURNE AND CAPE TOWN

LONGMANS, GREEN AND CO INC
55 FIFTH AVENUE NEW YORK 3

LONGMANS, GREEN AND CO
215 VICTORIA STREET TORONTO I

ORIENT LONGMANS LTD
BOMBAY CALCUTTA MADRAS

First published in 1953

PRINTED IN GREAT BRITAIN
BY WESTERN PRINTING SERVICES LTD, BRISTOL

PREFACE

THERE are already too many books about Sir Walter Ralegh. My only excuse for bringing out still one more is that the ground I wish to cover is rather different from that of previous works. I have tried to discuss Ralegh's literary and intellectual achievements and, by placing them in the context of his extraordinarily eventful life, to give some kind of conspectus of the whole man. My aim is to help the reader to perceive the manysidedness of Ralegh's attainments, not only because they are worth studying in themselves, but because Ralegh is a perfect reflection of the Renaissance imagination and a symbol of the English mind at a period when it was perhaps at its most alert and versatile.

Because I have wished to keep the balance between artist, thinker and man of action, it has been impossible to give Ralegh's writings as full a study as they require. Any discussion of the verse, for example, really demands a long survey of the extremely vexed questions of authorship and text. To know for certain what Ralegh wrote is a necessary prelude to a study of his poems. These problems of scholarship need an all-or-nothing treatment: within my present limits, my only choice has been 'nothing'. I have simply talked about those poems which I myself consider to be Ralegh's and which to my mind are worth talking about. An exception is one well-known lyric which I have tried to argue is by another hand. I omit problems of scholarship with a better conscience because there is easily available Miss A. M. C.

Latham's invaluable latest edition of Ralegh's poems (The Muses' Library, 1951). This contains the evidence a reader needs to make up his own mind on the Ralegh canon, and holds besides what is easily the best critical appreciation of the verse. My own debts to Miss Latham's scholarship are profound.

Again, it may seem a desperate enterprise to try to describe, within a single chapter, so full and rich a career as Ralegh's. Certainly I have had to present only the findings, and not all the complicated details, on such matters as the last voyage or the charges brought against Ralegh in 1603, and nowhere do I pretend to give more than an outline sketch. But so far as presenting a picture of the man's personality goes, I doubt if it would be possible to get much nearer to the 'real' Ralegh were all the space in the world at my disposal. The whole 'truth' about anyone long dead is inaccessible: assessment in biography is a partial and personal business. A good full-length biography will, of course, present the reader with all the material for making his own assessment; but in putting forward a personal view of Ralegh it seems to me a chapter may be as good as a long book.

In discussing Ralegh's religious and scientific outlook, I have paid rather scant attention to the story of the coterie which has been labelled 'The School of Night'. To have presented at length the evidence for and against, before arriving at my conclusion that it is improbable the 'School' existed, would, I think, have bored readers. There are several works in which the ground is fully covered by those who have more enthusiasm for the debate than I.

My debt to previous writers on Ralegh will be readily recognised. Of the biographies on which I have shamelessly drawn I have found Stebbing's still, after sixty years, the wisest and most ably-written. Professor D. B. Quinn's essay on Ralegh's colonial enterprises I have found constantly useful. Like everyone else who has written on Ralegh in recent years, I have drawn heavily on the mass of materials brought forward by Professor V. T. Harlow in his two books on the Guiana expeditions. Professor E. A. Strathmann's articles and his recent book on Ralegh's thought and *The History of the World* constitute the most serious study of the subject ever undertaken: I rarely dissent from the conclusions of his scholarship. My debt to Miss Latham's work I have already mentioned.

My quotations from *The History of the World* are taken from the third edition (1617), which T. N. Brushfield believed to have been revised by Ralegh. In these, as in all other quotations save those from Spenser, I have modernised the spelling and, where I thought the modern reader would be helped, altered the punctuation. The quotations from Ralegh's poetry are based upon Miss Latham's texts of 1929 and 1951. I have not, however, followed her in separating the quatrains of 'Cynthia' one from another, preferring to keep the arrangement of Ralegh's own manuscript.

Finally, a word about the pronunciation of the name Ralegh. Contemporaries spelt the name in a great variety of ways, but nearly always the first syllable is 'Raw-' or 'Rau-'. Ralegh himself used Rauley or Rawleyghe up to 1584: thenceforward consistently Ralegh. The accepted modern pronunciation (forgetting the popular 'Rally') has been, in view of the Elizabethan spelling, 'Rawly'. But Elizabethans would not have pronounced a word spelt with -*aw*- in the way we do. In the sixteenth century -*aw*- and -*au*- spellings would originally have indicated a sound like that of -*ow*- in *town*. But in the latter part of the century, the pronunciation was moving towards a sound like that of -a- in *father*. Elizabethan pronunciation is a complicated problem and it is impossible to be precise, but as a child Ralegh may still have pronounced his name 'Rowley'; as a middle-aged man he probably said 'Rahley'.

For a modern pronunciation, I suggest that 'Rowley' is unrecognisable, 'Rahley' is safe and sound, and 'Rawley', for those who are used to it, can be defended on the grounds that the spelling most often used in Elizabethan days would now be pronounced in that way.

ACKNOWLEDGMENTS

IT is a pleasure to acknowledge some of the courtesies I have met with in preparing this book. I am most grateful to the Marquess of Salisbury for his kindness in allowing me to examine the manuscript of *The Ocean to Cynthia*, and in permitting a photograph to be reproduced, and also to Mr. R. L. Drage, Curator of Hatfield House. Mr. W. F. Oakeshott generously gave his time showing me Ralegh's notebook for his *History* at Winchester. My thanks go to Mrs. E. E. Duncan-Jones, Mr. Philip Styles and Professor Kenneth Muir, who have read parts or the whole of the book at various stages and have made helpful suggestions. Professor A. S. C. Ross and Mr. E. G. Stanley kindly gave me information about Elizabethan pronunciation. I should like to express also my gratitude to Mr. Cyprian Blagden of Messrs. Longmans, Green and Co. for his encouragement, his patience and his valuable criticisms.

CONTENTS

ILLUSTRATIONS

Chapter One

THE LIFE

Early Years

RALEGH was born, probably in 1552, at Hayes Barton, near Budleigh Salterton, in Devon, of a family that had an honourable enough history though it could claim little distinction in the days of Ralegh's immediate forebears. His father was an independent and self-respecting gentleman and Ralegh was a younger son by his third wife, Katherine Gilbert (born Champernoun). He had as half-brothers (the children of his mother by her previous marriage) John, Humphrey and Adrian Gilbert, all of whom won renown at sea or on oversea adventures.

The first things known about Ralegh show him, not an adolescent, but beginning his career as a man. It seems that after a brief residence at Oxford, he made his way, in 1569, to join English volunteers fighting on the side of the Huguenots in the French religious wars. He had started his hunt for an occupation. As Sir Robert Naunton, his contemporary, put it: 'Being the youngest brother, and the house diminished in patrimony, he foresaw his own destiny: that he was first to roll (through want, and disability to subsist otherways) before he could come to a repose and, as the stone doth, by long lying, gather moss.' It was not in his father's power to help Ralegh beyond seeing him to the University and possibly assisting him later at the Inns of Court. He had to find his own feet and make his own fortune; he accepted the challenge, and in France we see him already embarked on a reconnaissance of life.

Civil wars were as vicious and merciless in the sixteenth century as in the twentieth. France at this time would be a harsh school of experience for a boy still in his 'teens, and Ralegh must have been campaigning for about five years (a period that takes in the Bartholomew massacres). He would have returned to England matured in many ways.

The year 1575 finds him at the Inns of Court and we know that two years after this Ralegh has obtained an introduction at the Court. But how he spent his time in London can only be guesswork. That he was writing verse is known from a sententious commendatory poem published at this time, which contains the prophetic couplet:

> For whoso reaps renown above the rest
> With heaps of hate shall surely be oppress'd.

It is worth bearing in mind that in these years in London Ralegh was laying the foundations of his wide reading and acquiring the intellectual and artistic interests that later marked him, because most of the legends about him as a young man present a rather different picture of him— as a wild and irresponsible youth. Ben Jonson, relating the story of a monstrous practical joke played upon him by Ralegh's son years later, tells that Lady Ralegh took the news of it in good part 'saying, his father young was so inclined'. John Aubrey, the seventeenth-century antiquary, who collected a great deal of material for Ralegh's life, says that 'in his youth his companions were boisterous blades, but generally those that had wit', and tells an anecdote of how Ralegh beat the egregious Charles Chester—'a bold impertinent fellow'—and sealed his

mouth with hard wax. For taking part in a brawl with
the courtier Sir Thomas Perrot, Ralegh was imprisoned
for a brief period. A young man of fashion, ambition
and talent, Ralegh pursued learning and life with equal
impetuosity.

After France and London, the sea. In his first sea
expedition of 1578, Ralegh was a principal in an expedition of Humphrey Gilbert's and commanded the *Falcon*.
Although the enterprise, directed towards Newfoundland and the North American coast in that region, was of
some importance historically in marking the beginnings
of the great attempt to settle Englishmen in transatlantic
colonies it achieved absolutely nothing. The fleet broke
up and Ralegh made a lonely six month cruise in the
Falcon seeking adventure and booty without success.

It was presumably owing to the favour of Humphrey
Gilbert, who had been much involved in Irish affairs,
that Ralegh owed his entry in a minor way into the
service of the Crown; he was given, in 1580, a commission as captain of a band of foot-soldiers to assist Lord
Grey of Wilton in the suppression of Desmond's rebellion
in Munster. There are many accounts of his courage and
ingenuity and the devotion of his subordinates. His
admiring fellow-countryman, the antiquary and leading
citizen of Exeter, John Hooker, tells the story of his
being surprised by an ambush at a ford and being greatly
outnumbered. His comrade Henry Moyle was unhorsed
in mid-stream and Ralegh went back to defend him with
pistol and quarterstaff while the rest of the little troop
crossed to safety.

But more sombre tales are told of Ralegh's ferocity
and his ruthlessness with the rebels. Once, a peasant
was taken prisoner and he had a bundle of withies; to
Ralegh's questioning what they were for, the man de-

fiantly replied 'To hang up the English churls with!' 'Is it so?' answered Ralegh, 'They shall now serve for an Irish kern.' And the man was hanged on the instant. Ralegh was at the siege of a fort in Smerwick Bay, which was held by 'a mongrel force' of Irishmen, and Spanish and Italian interventionists. The fort twice refused summonses to yield unconditionally to Lord Grey and, when the assault was successful, the Deputy, like Tamburlaine, ignored the foe's pleas for mercy. He sent in Ralegh and Mackworth, not because of their known cruelty, but because they had the ward of the day: 'Then put I in certain bands, who straight fell to execution.' Six hundred were slain, all the Irishmen being hanged and most of the Spaniards and Italians put to the sword. Stebbing says: 'The massacre excited general horror through Europe.' The Queen herself, according to Camden, could hardly be persuaded that the cruelty was justified. This holocaust was not Ralegh's responsibility but Grey's; how much guilt Ralegh must bear depends on one's attitude to the complex ethical problem involved in crimes committed under military orders. But Ralegh was presumably not averse from his task; ruthless suppression was all along the savage policy he supported for the 'pacification' of Ireland. Some have been puzzled by the contrast between this inhumanity and the enlightened and Christian attitude he showed in dealing with the native population of the American lands which he sought to bring under the Crown. It is not easy to solve this contradiction. Certainly the Irish, in his eyes, were rebels, and civil war was the worst of crimes for the Elizabethan: a crime against God as well as against man. Suppression might seem to him a matter of principle as well as policy. But so far as policy goes, Ralegh pithily condemns himself when, in his *Instructions to his Son*, he says 'Cruelty engendreth no other thing than hatred.' It must be added, though it does not excuse Ralegh, that an extraordinary bitterness towards the Irish, a feeling that they were a nation of irredeemable Calibans, was very widespread among Elizabethans.

Ralegh was restive in Ireland. The subservience of a minor commission did not sort with his notions of himself. 'I have spent some time here under the Deputy', he wrote to Leicester, 'in such poor place and charge as, were it not for that I knew him to be one of yours, I would disdain it as much as to keep sheep.' For a mere captain to write like this to Leicester is strange indeed. The act is in tune with letters to Walsingham himself, fulminating against Grey. Ralegh considers himself qualified to quarrel with Grey's strategy, and writes behind Grey's back to great ones at court whose ear he had previously gained, impressing himself all the time on their attention, taking it upon himself to propose different Irish policies and strategies from those taken by his commander. He went back to England in December 1581, and almost at once he is on a new footing altogether. Truly Bacon was no cynic but an accurate observer when he said that 'all rising to great place is by a winding stair'. And Grey might well, in vehement disgust, protest of 'Captain Rawley': 'For mine own part, I must be plain: I neither like his carriage nor his company.'

Grace and Favour

Ralegh now climbs swiftly and steadily into eminence and wealth through the favour of the Queen. With startling suddenness he changes from a captain in the Irish wars to the courtier most tenderly regarded by Elizabeth. Perhaps it did all start with Ralegh's spread-

ing his cloak in a 'plashy place' for his Sovereign to tread
upon: such a gesture would be like the man. But cloak
or no cloak, Ralegh pushed himself into notice and,
once noticed, his abilities were such as to insist on recognition. 'The truth is, she took him for a kind of
oracle,' says Naunton, and he is referring to Ralegh's
advice, not only on Irish strategy; Ralegh's ideas were
vigorous and independent over a wide range of subjects
and it cannot have been unexciting to listen to his
expressing them. Add to this the impressiveness of
bearing Ralegh owned, and it becomes no wonder that
the Queen singled him out. It is enough to quote
Naunton:

> He had in the outward man a good presence, in a handsome
> and well-compacted person; a strong natural wit and a
> better judgment, with a bold and plausible tongue, whereby
> he could set out his parts to the best advantage.

Ralegh was an unusual man and could not help becoming
prominent. The Queen took to him, and for years he
remained in the sunshine of her favour. He could hardly
hope that she would give him a fortune; but she helped
him to win one himself. He was, for example, granted
the lucrative (though troublesome) monopoly of licen-
sing wines and a monopoly for exporting broadcloth.
He began to acquire residences and estates when the use
of Durham House in the Strand was granted him, and
huge Irish estates followed. The conviction of Babington
provided him with large English possessions which the
conspirator forfeited. Elizabeth knighted him in 1584;
the most signal token of her esteem was to create him in
1587 Captain of the Guard. Ralegh took charge of a
large body of yeomen, became personally responsible for
the Queen's safety at all times and was expected to be

in close attendance on her. The Yeomen of the Guard, 'splendid, tall, strong men, like half-giants', as a German visitor described them, were clad in brilliant livery and, as E. P. Cheyney remarked, 'must have done much to give to the English Court at this time its reputation for magnificence'. No pay came out of the royal purse for the post except for the Captain's uniform yearly; 'six yards of tawney medley, at thirteen shillings and four-pence a yard, with a fur of black budge, rated at ten pounds: sum, fourteen pounds', ran the account for 1592. The position was one awarded to Ralegh as a personal favourite: he was never one of the Queen's advisers on State affairs.

Many of Ralegh's appointments and offices had to do with the West Country (and we must remember also that he was returned as one of the two members of Parliament for Devon in 1584, and sat in each succeeding Parliament, except in 1588, in Elizabeth's reign). His appointment as Lord Warden of the Stannaries in 1585 gave him control of the tin-mining in Devon and Cornwall; he was made Lieutenant of Cornwall and Vice-Admiral of Cornwall and Devon. Ralegh had a special affection for his own country and the people returned his affection. That 'he spake broad Devonshire to his dying day' testifies to his feelings. Richard Carew the antiquary dedicated to him his *Survey of Cornwall* 'as one of the common beholden', 'over whose persons', he wrote,

you carry a large, both martial and civil, command by your authority; but in whose hearts and loves you possess a far greater interest by your kindness. Your ears and mouth have ever been open to hear and deliver our grievances, and your feet and hands ready to go and work their redress.

The story of the return of the Great Carrack in 1592 shows well the affection and loyalty the men of his own country and his own followers had for him. When Ralegh was in the Tower (for reasons shortly to be discussed) a fleet including his own ships, which he himself had commanded, came into Dartmouth with the Portuguese carrack *Madre de Dios* in tow. She was a vast ship, heavily laden with treasure in jewels, spices, silk and so forth, 'the richest single prize ever taken'. The vultures fell upon her: everyone from sailors to shopkeepers began looting. Ralegh was fetched in haste, under guard, from the Tower to restore order and make certain of the Queen's share of the booty. Sir Robert Cecil, who had gone down ahead fearing that 'the birds be flown, for jewels, pearls and amber' and stopping all on the road who 'smelled of the prizes', wrote in wonderment of the effect of Ralegh's arrival. 'I assure you, Sir, his poor servants to the number of 140 goodly men, and all the mariners, came to him with such shouts and joy that I never saw a man more troubled to quiet them.' Order was restored by Ralegh and the Queen was secured 'more than ever a man presented to her Majesty as yet'.

Yet in spite of the affection of his own countrymen, Ralegh was in general a thoroughly unpopular man. In 1587, Sir Anthony Bagot could write of him as 'the best hated man in the world: in court, city and country'. Most of the unpopularity was due to spite and jealousy; when Naunton described Elizabeth's taking Ralegh for a 'kind of oracle', he added, 'which nettled them all'. And Ralegh continued to 'nettle' all who considered themselves better born, more able and more steady than the scintillating upstart. He rubbed salt in the wounded self-esteem of the court: humility was no part of his make-up, he cared not the least what the world thought of him, and took no trouble to conciliate those whom his eminence might offend. Ralegh's magnificence contained a large measure of pride—using the word in both its Elizabethan and modern senses: ambitiousness, arrogance and vanity. 'He was a tall, handsome and bold man,' said Aubrey, 'but his naeve [*sc.* flaw] was that he was damnable proud.' His vanity included the gorgeousness with which he surrounded himself; the legends of his luxury are absurd, but at least indicate the envy his personal adornment excited. We hear of a white suit with jewels 'to the value of three-score thousand pounds' and shoes alone so bedecked as to be worth more than 6,000 pieces of gold. Even during his long imprisonment in the Tower he would wear 'a velvet cap laced and a rich gown'. For his use at sea, he had made a 'fine cabin bed . . . having furniture of green silk and legs carved like dolphins, gilt with gold'.

His arrogance needs little comment: 'If in Ireland they think that I am not worth the respecting, they shall much deceive themselves. I am in place to be believed not inferior to any man, to pleasure or displeasure the greatest; and my opinion is so received and believed as I can anger the best of them', he once wrote in high rage. We have already seen and shall see again his indifference to concealing the scorn he felt for those whose opinions he despised. The conventionally-minded exasperated him; he carried his undoubted distinction of mind without a trace of gentleness or modesty, or even condescension, towards those of inferior capacity. And among his intellectual peers he could not be at peace. 'He could never be connected with an enterprise which he was not determined to direct', says Stebbing, and his own close acquaintance, the Earl of Northumberland, remarked that 'he desired to seem to

be able to sway all men's fancies, all men's courses.'
A rival was always an enemy; Ralegh and the brilliant and
capricious Essex were at daggers drawn from the start
(though Essex fanned the flames of discord far more than
Ralegh). Essex, and the popular acclaim he always
received, reminds us that Ralegh never sought popularity
with the mob and, outside the West Country, never won
it without seeking. He was quite indifferent to his unpopularity, and let them sing in the streets the ballad
about him which runs:

> Ralegh doth time bestride,
> He sits 'twixt wind and tide,
> Yet uphill he cannot ride
> For all his bloody pride.

The New World

Ralegh looked for his main income not to the offices
and endowments given him by the Queen but to privateering and colonising. His own sea-exploits are of no
importance in the 1580's; he often planned to go on
a foray or a voyage of discovery only to be restrained
from setting out by the Queen, anxious not to lose him
in the way Sir Humphrey Gilbert was lost. But Ralegh's
mind and purse were behind many expeditions. He followed Sir Humphrey Gilbert in looking towards the
North American coastline for colonial exploitation,
though the latitudes that interested him were more
southerly and temperate. In March 1584, Ralegh acquired
a patent authorising him to search out and take possession
of, for himself and his heirs, 'remote, heathen and bar-
barous lands', not actually possessed by any Christian
prince. A reconnaissance of two ships which he sent
out brought back almost ecstatic reports of an earthly

paradise, for its rich soil and friendly inhabitants, in the region where they made a landfall, off the coast of what is now North Carolina. Ralegh at once began preparations for settling the land. Naming the territory Virginia was thought to be a tactful move in gaining the Queen's blessing; Hakluyt wrote a tract on the importance of colonising America; promoters and investors were looked for. Since returns were extremely speculative, Ralegh encouraged investors by combining privateering projects with his colonial plans—and he himself, of course, was as interested in the profits from privateering as from colonisation. This first colonial scheme was conceived in terms of capitalism. 'There is no mention of grants of lands to intending settlers. They were intended to work together as paid servants of the investors, under the commander whom Ralegh appointed. Probably, they were promised good wages and a share in profits, but the results of their labours in America were to go to pay the promoters.'[1] A fleet of seven ships was ready in April, 1585. Sir Richard Grenville took charge of the expedition. He left the settlers on Roanoke Island, and on his way home acquired enough treasure by piracy to ensure the perfect contentment of the promoters.

In the twelve months that followed, these first colonists did not really sink their roots. They explored and made experiments with crops; John White sketched and made maps, Thomas Harriot, the indefatigable scientist of the expedition, carried on his remarkable researches into native customs and natural history; but they took no determined steps to make themselves self-supporting with a properly organised agriculture, or to come to a satisfactory *modus vivendi* with the natives. Conditions grew worse between the settlers and the Indians until

[1] D. B. Quinn, *Raleigh and the British Empire*, p. 65.

there was a state of armed conflict. When Sir Francis Drake's fleet made its pre-arranged visit to the colony in June, 1586, the settlers, in sudden and somewhat panic-stricken fashion, asked to be taken home. When Grenville arrived a little later, he was bewildered to find no colonists, and he could get no word from the natives of what had happened to them. Anxious that Ralegh's schemes should not collapse, he left 15 men with abundant stores on Roanoke; they were set on by the natives and no one knows what eventually became of them.

Thus dishearteningly ended Ralegh's first colony. But he did not waver in his determination to gain a permanent foothold on the American continent, though it was naturally harder than ever to extract capital from the wealthy. A fresh scheme was prepared on a different principle; families were to be settled on their own land in a self-governing community. 150 householders under the command of John White left in early 1587. The colony's story is consistently unhappy. White came back for further supplies and was held up in England for various reasons until 1591. When, finally, he did return, he found a deserted settlement, chests and chattels buried, and carvings on trees which told that the settlers had moved, but not under duress. But what had become of them is utter mystery: they were not seen or heard of again.

After this succession of failures, Ralegh tried no more. But it must be said that when, in his lifetime, a successful colony was planted in Virginia, it was really a triumph for Ralegh's vision and protracted pioneering, and his great expense of energy. Ralegh led the way in settling Englishmen in the New World.

Meanwhile, there was a safer and more lucrative field of colonial enterprise in Ireland, and Ralegh, who had been granted big Irish estates in 1586–7, spent a great deal of time developing them and settling English families there, besides exploiting the natural resources with newly set-up industries. It was to his Irish estates that he came disconsolately in 1589, obviously under some sort of cloud, relieving his discontentment by means of poetry and the society of Edmund Spenser.

In 1592, Ralegh was ready with a new venture, this time a punitive expedition to strike at Spanish power in Panama. He prosecuted the venture with great vigour and expense but the Queen was again anxious to prevent his leading the fleet in person. Her favour towards Ralegh had been a little uncertain of late, but that it was steady at this moment is clear from her granting him the lease of Sherborne in Dorset, and from this concern for his safety. Ralegh reluctantly promised only to lead the fleet out and then to transfer his command to Frobisher. During the weeks that followed his return on May 9th, the Queen's feelings towards Ralegh veered from affection to high anger and resentment; in July, Ralegh was her prisoner in the Tower, in company with Elizabeth Throckmorton, one of Elizabeth's maids of honour. What it was precisely that so aroused the Queen's wrath is most obscure. Cecil spoke smugly of Ralegh's 'brutish offence'; all we really know is that at some point Ralegh married Elizabeth Throckmorton. Camden wrote that he had seduced her, and this view is accepted by Ralegh's best biographers: the eighteenth-century Oldys, who is highly amused by the story, and the nineteenth-century Stebbing, who is bewildered and hurt. There is certainly nothing improbable about Ralegh's deflowering a maid of honour, but it is dubious if such an escapade could be the full cause of the Queen's displeasure. It is now more generally supposed that it was a clandestine marriage that so upset the Queen, rather than a seduction of one to whom Elizabeth saw herself as moral guardian. In the Queen's eyes, Ralegh had no right to bestow his affection elsewhere than on her. To have made, secretly, the firmest possible declaration of affection to another was high insult and profound deceit. Elizabeth's almost pathological rage at the marriage of Essex is well-known. The marriage of a favourite was the strongest affront to her.

Ralegh's marriage, which began so inauspiciously, was most happy. Whether the relations between the two were in the first place sanctified by marriage is unimportant; if they were not, the kind of flippant seduction suggested by Oldys is by no means to be conjectured; Ralegh and Elizabeth seem to have loved each other deeply, and the story of their love through prosperity and adversity is moving indeed. When he was expecting execution in after years, Ralegh wrote to his wife: 'Remember your poor child for his father's sake, that chose you and loved you in his happiest time.'

In the Tower, Ralegh wrote the great poem of lament to the Queen which must be considered in its place. The imprisonment lasted only a month or two, but the Queen's displeasure endured for years, during which time Ralegh and his wife were banished the Court. He lived much at Sherborne, his 'fortune's fold', but sat in the Commons when Parliament met, proffered gratuitous advice to Burghley and his son on Irish affairs, carried on his own Irish enterprises, scandalised local clerics by his outspokenness on theological matters, captured a 'notable stout villain' of a Jesuit, was busy with Stannary Court affairs, and always, of course, had 'no other desire but to serve her Majesty'. 'The body is wasted with toil, the purse with charge, and all things worn.

Only the mind is indifferent to good fortune or adversity.' Besides thus practising stoicism (or professing it; some of the letters of this period are full of querulous passion) Ralegh was busily engaged in making plans to exploit a yet more profitable paradise than Virginia.

Guiana had interested Ralegh for many years. For a long time he had been collecting and sifting information about the legendary El Dorado, or Manoa: a civilization on the borders of a huge lake in the heart of the land through which the Orinoco flowed, where men anointed themselves with turpentine and coated themselves with gold-dust. To find this land, to annex it for the Queen, to exploit its wealth, was an enterprise to quicken the imagination and offer hope of a return of honour and profit to one sadly in need of them. In 1594, Ralegh sent Captain Whiddon to the Orinoco on a reconnaissance. Lady Ralegh tried to stop this madness on the part of her husband; she wrote to Cecil beseeching him not to 'help him forward toward the sunset'. But nothing could have restrained Ralegh. Whiddon brought back sanguine reports; Ralegh was given a Royal Commission to discover and subdue heathen lands; he raised all the money he could (Howard and Cecil making their contributions) to equip an expedition, and in February, 1595, he led out a squadron of four ships to make an extensive preliminary investigation of Guiana.

By the side of the extraordinary feats of the Spaniards in exploring Guiana in the face of terrible hardships, Ralegh's penetration of the Orinoco falls into place as a minor probe into comparatively well-known territory. Nevertheless, the account he himself gave of his journey makes a superb adventure story. After a successful affray in Trinidad with Berreo and his Spaniards, Ralegh was ready to begin his reconnaissance. To enable him to traverse the shoals and shallows he had an 'old galego' stripped and cut down into a galley of five feet draught, with oars, able to carry on the bottom boards 60 men and their provisions. Two wherries, a barge and a ship's boat made up the rest of the little squadron which left Trinidad and made an entry into one of the many mouths of the Orinoco. For weeks these boats were the homes of a hundred men:

> being all driven to lie in the rain and weather, in the open air, in the burning sun, and upon the hard boards, and to dress our meat and to carry all manner of furniture in them, wherewith they were so pestered and unsavoury, that what with victuals being most fish, with the wet clothes of so many men thrust together and the heat of the sun, I will undertake there was never any prison in England that could be found more unsavoury and loathsome, especially to myself who had for many years before been dieted and cared for in a sort far differing.

Ralegh said that when the men began to tire and despair, he cheered them on with false accounts of the nearness of their destination, but the fact that they endured the arduous journey as long as they did must mean that he had finer means of inspiring their loyalty than deceit.

To gain the friendship of the natives wherever he went was a fundamental aim of Ralegh's. The Spaniards had looted, captured, killed and tortured mercilessly, and had reaped their reward in the permanent and deadly hostility of the natives. As a matter both of policy and of principle, Ralegh wanted the friendship of the inhabitants, and he spared no pains to conciliate them and to win their confidence. This task could have been more difficult; Ralegh found a ready audience when he announced himself as the sworn foe of the Spaniard. He confirmed his protestations that he came only for the good of the natives by utterly forbidding his men to interfere with the women or take any loot:

> I suffered not any man to take from any of the nations so much as a Pina or a Potato root, without giving them contentment, nor any man so much as to offer to touch any of their wives or daughters; which course, so contrary to the Spaniard's (who tyrannise over them in all things) drew them to admire her Majesty, whose commandment I told them it was, and also wonderfully to honour our nation.

He confesses, however, that it was 'a very impatient work to keep the meaner sort from spoil and stealing'. The friendship of the natives was important also as a means of gaining information the more readily. Everywhere he found 'confirmation' of what he sought—that somewhere to the south-west there was an opulent civilisation, as rich as Peru. So successfully did Ralegh impress himself on the natives as their friend and liberator, that the tribes of Guiana still spoke of him and looked for his return 150 years later.

Ralegh began to build up his chart of the Orinoco basin, its natural features and its inhabitants, everything being food for his keen observation, from the marital customs of the tribes to alligators and armadillos. And always, of course, his eyes were greedy for signs of gold. So great was his faith in the mineral richness of Guiana, that every hill and the very ground sparkled their promise of wealth to him.

It took the party 15 days to reach the main stream of the Orinoco, and even in that time food had become short and the men dispirited. Once their guide persuaded Ralegh to enter a side-stream with a small party, on the promise of meeting a friendly tribe and replenishing their food supplies. As they went further and further away from the main body, they began to fear a trap:

At the last we determined to hang the pilot, and if we had well known the way back again by night, he had surely gone; but our own necessities pleaded sufficiently for his safety, for it was as dark as pitch, and the river began so to narrow itself, and the trees to hang over from side to side, as we were driven with arming swords to cut a passage thorough those branches that covered the water . . . It was now eight o'clock at night and our stomachs began to gnaw apace . . . The poor old Indian ever assured us that it was but a little farther, and but this one turning, and that turning, and at last, about one o'clock after midnight, we saw a light, and rowing towards it we heard the dogs of the village.

Thereafter all was well; there was food to store, and they discovered themselves in a terrain rich and beautiful, where 'the deer came down feeding by the water's side, as if they had been used to a keeper's call'.

The going was easier when they reached the main stream of the Orinoco, and they went on, refreshing themselves with such delicacies as turtles' eggs, marvelling at the novelties of the scenery, making contact with the chieftains of the various tribes, until they came to the river Caroni, at whose source Ralegh had understood the lake of Manoa to lie. It was impossible to row against the current of the Caroni, so three land parties were made up. Towards the mighty waterfalls of the Caroni, Ralegh found another paradise: 'the deer crossing in every path, the birds towards the evening singing on every tree with a thousand several tunes, cranes and herons of white, crimson and carnation perching on the river's side, the air fresh with a gentle easterly wind, and every stone that we stooped to take up promised either gold or silver by his complexion.' From the rocky ground with daggers and fingers they prised out samples of ore that were later pronounced by London assayers to be indeed gold-bearing.

But it was impossible to stay longer. The rainy season was beginning. 'The river began to rage and overflow very fearfully, and the rains came down in terrible showers, and gusts in great abundance.' The men began to cry out and Ralegh, anxious about removing himself further from his base when he knew that Spanish reinforcements were expected at Trinidad, decided it was time to return. The journey down-stream was infinitely less laborious; a great deal of exploration was carried out. Being a poor walker, Ralegh left excursions on foot to Laurence Keymis, who went inland with a chieftain who promised gold. When the parties were reunited, this chieftain, Putijma, 'offered to send his son with us into England, if we could have staid till he had sent back to his town. But our hearts were cold to behold the great rage and increase of Orenoque, and therefore departed and turned toward the west.' Eventually, the hazards of the delta successfully overcome, the adventurers reached Trinidad 'where we found our ships at anchor, than which there was never to us a more joyful sight'.

This voyage to Guiana brought Ralegh neither fortune nor reinstatement. He found on every hand, on his return, scepticism about the genuineness of the specimens of ore he brought back, or rumours that, if the gold were genuine, he had got it from less inaccessible and distant places than Guiana. His indignation at this reception shows itself in his published narrative. 'I am not so much in love with these long voyages as to devise thereby to cozen myself: to lie hard, to fare worse, to be subjected to perils, to diseases, to ill savours, to be parched and withered and withal to sustain the care and labour of such an enterprise, except the same had more comfort than the fetching of marcasite in Guiana, or buying of gold ore in Barbary.' His whole account, *The Discovery of the*

Large, Rich and Beautiful Empire of Guiana, is a piece of propaganda, designed to stir the hearts of the unconvinced with a prospect of undreamed-of riches, and to suggest the exploitation of Guiana as a practical proposition. But Elizabeth and the city merchants remained sceptical. For the moment Ralegh had to be content with the help of Burghley and Cecil in sending back Keymis with a small expedition. Keymis discovered that the Spaniards had already tightened their hold on the country with reinforcements and had built a settlement near the mouth of the Caroni. His efforts to reach the Caroni mine were frustrated, and once again, he did not achieve a sight of the second gold mine by the mountain Iconuri.

Cadiz and the Islands Voyage

It was not long after the anti-climax of his return from Guiana that Ralegh was on his way back to favour through his bearing in the Cadiz voyage. Ralegh's policy towards Spain had been an unwearied *delenda est*. Over the years he had warned his countrymen in print, in private letters, in conversation, of the danger of Spanish power and the fixity of Spanish malevolence towards England, and he would have been well pleased when Elizabeth was frightened into giving her consent at last to a large-scale punitive action against Spain. In June, 1596, a fighting fleet and its train to the number of about 120 ships set sail carrying an army of about 10,000 men. Howard and Essex were in command; Ralegh had a naval command of 22 ships. The fleet made for Cadiz and surprised a big Spanish concentration of four great galleons and many galleys and merchantmen. The value of surprise was lost, however, when Essex proceeded to load the soldiers into boats in accordance with the agreed plan of first taking the town; the water was dangerously rough, and Ralegh returned from a reconnaissance along the coast to find boats capsizing and soldiers drowning. He immediately went aboard Essex's ship, persuaded him of the folly of the enterprise, and won consent for the alternative plan of entering first with the fleet.

Ralegh was determined to have no rivals in the honour of leading the attack against the ships which now had time to retire further into the harbour and prepare their defence. 'With the first peep of day, therefore, I weighed anchor and bare with the Spanish fleet, taking the start of all ours a good distance.' Ralegh's own account of the action in a letter to an unknown friend is exciting and vivid. He sailed magnificently past the galleys, answering their salvoes with blasts of a trumpet, until the shot fell a little too close, when he 'bestowed a benediction amongst them'. He sailed up to confront the ranged galleons and anchored by them; the set battle began, and lasted until 10 at night. A horrifying spectacle it must have been, this fierce fight between two fleets in the narrow neck of the harbour. After three hours of furious bombardment, Ralegh feared he might sink, and sought permission from Essex to board. But as soon as the Spaniards saw the preparations being made, they slipped their anchors and ran themselves aground, 'tumbling into the sea heaps of soldiers, so thick, as if coals had been poured out of a sack, in many ports at once, some drowned, and some sticking in the mud'. Two of the galleons fired themselves, and 'if any man had a desire to see Hell itself, it was there most lively figured'.

The subsequent storming and taking of the town and the tremendous sack of Cadiz belong to Essex's story rather than to Ralegh's, for Ralegh had been wounded in the leg and could take no part. Such was the eagerness

for plunder that the English ships were deserted; the
Spanish merchant fleet was able to fire itself, and the
galleys to escape to the open sea. Ralegh complained
bitterly of missing his share of the splendid loot, but he
did not do too badly: his share of the spoils was valued
at £1,769; he acquired a chest of books, and from a more
active despoiler he won at gaming 'five little pieces of
wrought plate'.

Cadiz was a great personal triumph for Ralegh as it was
a great national triumph for England. One of Essex's
faction, far from being predisposed to like Essex's hated
rival, generously admitted that 'Sir Walter Ralegh did in
my judgment no man better . . . I never knew the gentleman until this time, and I am sorry for it, for there are in
him excellent things beside his valour; and the observation he hath in this voyage used with my lord of Essex
hath made me love him.' It was less easy to convince the
Queen again of Ralegh's worth, but as the months went
by her animosity was clearly lessening; no doubt the
patching up of the Ralegh-Essex feud through Cadiz
helped. At any rate, on 1 June, 1597, nearly a year after
the action, 'Cynthia' allowed 'the Ocean' to resume in
person his office of Captain of the Guard.

The only other sea-exploit in which Ralegh was to
shine was of this period, during the inglorious Islands
Voyage. Essex, Ralegh and Cecil were for the moment a
triumvirate united in their policy of aggression toward
Spain. A punitive expedition was planned by them to
destroy the mobilized Spanish fleet and operate against
the Azores. Protracted preparations and recurrent
delays made a bad start to an expedition whose whole
story is one of vacillation and mismanagement. The
fleet that eventually sailed in August 1597 had Essex
as commander-in-chief, Lord Thomas Howard as vice-

admiral and Ralegh as rear-admiral and member of the council-of-war. The Spanish fleet was to be attacked in Ferrol, but Ferrol was left unmolested while the English followed a wild-goose-chase off to the Azores. Then a plan was made for Essex and Ralegh to take Fayal. Ralegh's squadron arrived off the town before Essex, who was cruising aimlessly. Ralegh waited about in the roads and had the galling sight of the inhabitants moving their goods and treasures inland. At last he decided that to wait any longer for Essex would destroy all hope of a successful raid and so he made a landing. He himself led his men against an opposition that was at first formidable, and won his way to the fort and occupied the town. Ralegh's strike was the only success of the whole expedition, but, alas for his pains! when Essex arrived the next day, out of temper after a fruitless chase, he was furious to find himself cheated of a chance of honour. He charged Ralegh with insubordination in making an attack in his absence, without his permission. The Earl's satellites talked of court-martials and executions. Ralegh vehemently insisted that, as a principal commander, it was lawful for him to act on his own initiative, considering the circumstances. Essex's wrath cooled quickly and he was willing to apologise, and the fleet got ready for its next blunder—the failure to intercept the vastly rich West Indian treasure fleet, which sailed safely into harbour at Terceira.

Prosperity and Ruin, 1598–1603

Essex's decline dates from the failure of the Islands Voyage, and Essex's decline meant Ralegh's ascent. For a few years now, until his own downfall, Ralegh was a power in the land. He gained no official position, nor was he attended by any such popularity as clung to his rival Essex even in the latter's flaming career earthwards, but he had authority. In the rivalry with Essex, the malice was never on Ralegh's side. Essex could descend to absurd pettiness as on the occasion of a tournament before the Queen in November, 1598. He appeared in the field with a huge retinue in the very colours which Ralegh had chosen for *his* band—presumably to swamp Ralegh's show, and give Ralegh and his men the appearance of being merely followers of Essex. But by the very fact that Essex hated him, Ralegh's destruction was being prepared for him, for to be Essex's foe was to be the foe of James of Scotland. The story that it was Ralegh who engineered the death of Essex was embroidered down to such details as that during the Earl's execution he had scornfully puffed away at a pipe.

In 1601, Ralegh took his seat in Parliament as usual. The role he played in the House of Commons was a distinguished one; E. P. Cheyney remarks that if nothing else had contributed to his renown, he would still have been famous as one of the most active parliament men of his time. Some of his speeches show a rather truculent nationalism, and not always against Spain. When, for example, a bill to restrain Dutchmen from setting up as tradesmen in England came up for debate, Ralegh's powerful oratory helped to carry it against those who, like Shakespeare's Sir Thomas More, argued against the 'momtanish inhumanyty' of refusing asylum to foreign refugees, and pleaded for Englishmen to do as they would be done by:

> What country, by the nature of your error,
> Should give *you* harbour?

But Ralegh could show greater humanity and, indeed, great wisdom. In 1593, he spoke against measures to punish nonconformity among the Brownists. He had no wish to countenance puritanism, he said, but

> what danger may grow to ourselves if this law pass, it were fit to be considered. For it is to be feared that men not guilty will be included in it, and that law is hard that taketh life and sendeth into banishment, where men's intentions shall be judged by a jury, and they shall be judges what another means.

For all his unpopularity with the people, Ralegh worked in Parliament to maintain the interests of the less fortunate, and when subsidies were debated, for example, he spoke vehemently against the suggestion that the poorer classes should be taxed in the same way as richer men.

In spite of Ralegh's great influence after the execution of Essex, he never came nearer to an official position of authority than being made Governor of Jersey. Elizabeth's chief counsellor was Cecil. Cecil and Ralegh had been intimate friends for years, but, with the end of Elizabeth's reign clearly not far away, Cecil was eager to make such arrangements with James of Scotland as would secure for the nation a tranquil and orderly succession and for himself a safe position under the new monarch. This meant the end of his friendship with one who might be a dangerous rival. Ralegh's own attitude to the succession is far from clear: one legend that should not be dismissed out of hand is that he favoured a republic. At any rate, he also played his part in the unsavoury jockeying for position; he had two most unsafe allies in Henry Brooke, Lord Cobham, and the Catholic Earl of Northumberland; for safety's sake he had, like all the rest, his lines of communication with the Scottish court. There, however, he and Cobham had little chance against the calumny of Cecil's ally Henry Howard. It is possible that Cecil had no knowledge of Howard's quite dastardly correspondence, which, in the months before the death of Elizabeth, succeeded in poisoning James's mind against Ralegh beyond all hope of cure. He delighted in pouring into James's willing ear his venom about the 'atheism' of 'those wicked villains': 'Hell did never vomit up such a couple.' Even Cecil could stoop to such descriptions as 'those gaping crabs'. Ralegh had no inkling of the crevasse before him. How should he? Ten weeks before the Queen's death, Cecil could write amicably to him about preparations for a privateering exploit in which he, Ralegh and Cobham were partners.

Queen Elizabeth died on 24 March, 1603. Within four months Ralegh was arrested and held while charges of treason were prepared against him. Even before James reached London, his determination to strip Ralegh of all power and consequence was made quite clear. By reducing Ralegh, James was killing two birds with one stone. He was not only disarming a dangerous man, but helping his own bid for popularity by humiliating a thoroughly unpopular one. Honours and possessions were peeled from him; he was relieved of his dearly prized office of Captain of the Guard and deprived of his London residence, Durham House. But still he could not see what lay in store from him; Ralegh was even hopeful enough to imagine that the new King might be more favourable to the idea of a war against Spain than the old Queen, and, quite incredibly, laid before the pacific James plans for aggression against the old enemy.

How his enemies enmeshed Ralegh in the web of treason is a long and complicated story which cannot be gone into here. All centres on Cobham, who had foolishly flirted with Spain by entering into negotiations with D'Aremberg, minister of the rulers of the Netherlands. Ralegh, while waiting on the Terrace at Windsor to follow the King's hunt one day in July, was ordered by Cecil to stay to be questioned by the Lords on his knowledge of these negotiations. The plots in which evidence was sought to implicate Ralegh and Cobham were the 'Bye' plot—to surprise and abduct the King, and the 'Main' plot—to substitute Arabella Stuart for James. Cobham's behaviour was extraordinary. He was examined and eventually cried out, on learning that Ralegh had admitted some knowledge of Cobham's correspondences, that he had entered upon them only at Ralegh's instigation. On the strength of this wild accusation Ralegh was committed to the Tower, and his lieutenant Keymis also arrested and questioned. Resignation from the wardenship of the Stannaries was exacted from him, and a little later his Governorship of Jersey was declared forfeit.

A tremendous search for tangible evidence against Ralegh began, but there was nothing to build on except hearsay, the undoubted fact that Ralegh *was* 'discontented', and Cobham's bare assertion. But at last Ralegh could see where he stood. The absurdity of the situation would be sinister enough indication how grave his plight was. He, the life-long and implacable foe of Spain, was to be accused of being in treasonable correspondence with her through Cobham! (And in any case much of Cobham's negotiations with D'Aremberg had been in the cause so much at James's heart—peace.) Throughout his life Ralegh had made enemies at court and now he saw himself reaping the harvest of accumulated malice; he knew only too well that he could not look for justice, and he is reported to have tried to take his own life. At last Cobham's conscience began to torment him and Ralegh, who had contrived to smuggle a note to him beseeching him to speak the truth, won from him letters entirely acquitting him of the base charges of complicity. But Ralegh had already been indicted, and a day or two afterwards was on his way to Winchester to be tried for his life.

Nothing became Ralegh like his conduct at his trial on 17 November. On his way to Winchester he had to pass through a mob so hostile that his keeper thought they were lucky to get through unscathed. His trial changed all that, and in his ruination he achieved the popular respect and sympathy he had never known in the days of his prosperity. One who witnessed his trial said: 'Never was a man so hated and so popular in so short a time.' And another told the King that although at the outset 'he was so led with the common hatred that he would have gone a hundred miles to see him hanged, he would, ere they parted, have gone a thousand to save his life'. After all these years it is still a stirring experience to read the record of the trial. Amazement at the flimsiness of the evidence, anger at the malice of the accusers, bewilderment at the partisanship of the judges, admiration for the dignity and spirit of the accused and pity for his plight, distress that such things can be—all these emotions succeed one other in us as we follow the story of a trial concerning which one of the presiding judges confessed in later years: 'Never was English justice so injured, so degraded.'

Ralegh pleaded Not Guilty to the charge of contriving with Cobham, with the help of Spain, to supplant the King and enthrone Arabella Stuart. The prosecution, in the hands of Coke, was an amplification (in tragic terms) of Dogberry's words, 'Masters, it is proved

already that you are little better than false knaves, and it
will go near to be thought so shortly'. A mass of irrele-
vant details was punctuated with such ejaculations as
'Thou art a monster: thou hast an English face, but a
Spanish heart', ' . . . this viper . . .', 'Thou hast a Spanish
heart, and thyself art a spider of hell.' The whole 'case'
was built around Cobham's accusation of Ralegh. Re-
peatedly, Ralegh demanded that his accuser should be
brought to the court to testify:

> If I have done these things I deserve not to live, whether they
> be treasons by the law or no. I beseech you then, my Lords,
> let Cobham be sent for . . . If he will then maintain his
> accusation to my face, I will confess myself guilty.

> Good my lords, let my accuser come face to face.

> Vouchsafe me but this grace: Let him be brought, being
> alive and in the house hard by, let him avow any of these
> speeches, and I will confess the whole indictment.

Ralegh had based his claims on law: that two witnesses
were needed in a charge of treason, and that they must
testify in person. When they refused him this, he demanded confrontation with his accuser in the name of
decency and common justice. He spoke with the courage, logic and dignity of a man confident in his own inno-
cence; he was met with the prevarications, hot temper,
bad logic and special pleading of men who knew that
their case depended upon keeping the unstable Cobham
out of court. The measure of the legal arguments that
were opposed against Ralegh's only too reasonable
demand lies in the revealing remark that the Chief
Justice of England, Popham, let slip *after Ralegh had been
found guilty*, in the passing of sentence: 'It now comes
into my mind, why you may not have your accuser face
to face . . .' Well might Ralegh, in a moment of despair

during the trial, cry out: 'If this may be, you will have any man's life in a week.' There *was* one witness produced, a seaman who had heard a fellow say in Portugal that Cobham and Ralegh would cut James's throat. 'What infer you upon that?' asked Ralegh wearily. 'That your treason hath wings,' replied Coke!

Ralegh had not realised the depths of Cobham's perfidy. His trump-card was the latter's recantation that he had surreptitiously secured. But Coke suddenly produced a new statement by Cobham of his charges against Ralegh, written after the recantation. 'Ralegh was much amazed', says the reporter, but 'by and by he seemed to gather his spirits again' and produced the letter of acquittal. But it was of no use; there was no one in court interested in showing him justice. He had pleaded his past service in vain and his lifelong hostility towards Spain; there was no-one in court interested in showing him mercy. He was convicted before he appeared in the court. The intimidated jury took only 15 minutes to bring in a verdict of Guilty, and Popham, in a speech of gloating malevolence, gave judgment, ending with the horrible sentence of being hanged, drawn and quartered. It is perhaps worth mentioning that in a few months' time, when James had made peace with Spain, four of the judges who had condemned Ralegh for his correspondence with that country received secret pensions from the Spanish Ambassador.[1]

With savage suddenness, Ralegh had been reduced from one at the height of his power, with a future rich with potentialities to a prisoner in the Tower awaiting execution. But he was not to be executed. For reasons that are obscure, James granted Ralegh his life. Little else but his life was left him. What remained of his offices dis-

[1] E. Thompson, *Sir Walter Ralegh* (1935), pp. 201–2.

appeared, and even Sherborne, which it seemed at one time might be saved for his wife and child, was taken from him.

The Tower and the Last Voyage

During his twelve years' incarceration in the Tower, Ralegh aged rapidly and was constantly in ill-health. But he contrived some sort of a home for himself and his wife, and their second son, Carew, was born in the precincts. The existence he led was a remarkable one, bearing the unique stamp of his personality and imagination. He turned a hut into a laboratory, he entertained Harriot and other scholars, he held conversations with his fellow-prisoner, the 'Wizard' Earl of Northumberland, he built model ships for Prince Henry and prepared medical prescriptions for the Queen herself; more important than all, he conceived, prepared and began that vast work, impossible of achievement, his *History of the World*: a copy of the only volume to be published, a thick folio, now rests in a show-case in the Bloody Tower, a monument to an unquenchable spirit.

His activities must have vexed James sorely. He wrote discourses against the marriages proposed for the royal children; he won not only the Queen's sympathy, but Prince Henry's firm friendship ('Who but my father would keep such a bird in a cage?'). Young Prince Henry listened eagerly to and encouraged the schemes he heard from Sir Walter: schemes about navigation, about Guiana, about the folly of temporising with Spain, about writing the history of the world. The Prince's death in 1612 at the age of 18, a great misfortune for England, was an unhappy event for Ralegh, for, besides a friend and admirer, he lost the only person who might have had the will and the power to secure his release.

Something of the quality of the hope that persisted in Ralegh may be seen in his attitude to Guiana. He somehow managed to send ships to maintain contact with the land and the natives he had promised to come back to. In his confinement, Guiana became a talisman to end all his wretchedness; he dwelt upon the promise of the country until the picture of what was became the vision of what might be—the winning of freedom to sail away and establish what had been only begun in 1595, and to bring back to James enough gold to buy his pardon and set himself up once more in estate and position. In the years 1610, 1611 and 1612, Ralegh was petitioning the Queen and the Lords to send him to the New World. He promised gold—not the gold of El Dorado (which he wisely and conveniently forgot) but gold from the mines from which in 1595 he had brought back specimens of ore. But it was not until 1616 that Ralegh's constant dangling of riches and territorial acquisition before the eyes of authority began to take effect. James was still dallying with Spain, but he was also in urgent need of money; in addition, the new Secretary of State, Sir Ralph Winwood, was no friend to Spain and in no way troubled at the thought of possible friction between the two countries should England make a bid for Guiana gold. In March, 1616, Ralegh was granted a conditional release to make preparations for a voyage to Guiana. Gaining this freedom was his last victory.

There is an air of madness about this last gamble of Ralegh's. There is something hectic and wild-eyed about him and at the same time something of the grim coldness of desperation. The prudent weighing of consequences was the last thing he permitted himself. As we follow the hopeless and sorry endeavour, we have to wing our imaginations and try to enter into Ralegh's mood and

situation if we are to give his story a sympathetic understanding.

James's conduct it is not easy to see in a favourable
light. He was divided between an anxiety not to irritate
Spain and greed for what Ralegh might win. He knew
as well as anyone that the Spaniards considered Guiana
their territory, that a Spanish settlement, San Thomé,
had been set up on the banks of the Orinoco and that if
Ralegh went, there was bound to be a collision. James
was prepared to risk Spanish anger, were Ralegh to succeed and open up an inexhaustible treasure-store in
Guiana. So he listened to Ralegh's explanations that
Guiana was territory which he, Ralegh, had annexed for
England in 1595, and that territorial aggression was therefore not in question. Such arguments might be useful for
the future. On the other hand, Ralegh might fail : and so
James protected himself with all the duplicity of which he
was capable by arranging a very heavy insurance. The
irate Spanish ambassador Gondomar he plied with soft
answers. From Ralegh he exacted an undertaking not to
invade Spanish territory or to injure Spanish vassals—an
undertaking Ralegh can only have given in the belief that
James accepted his contention that the Spaniards had no
official right in Guiana. Ralegh was carefully left unpardoned. Full information on the size of Ralegh's fleet,
its routes and destination were supplied to Gondomar
for transmission to Madrid. If Ralegh failed to win for
him wealth and power enough to free him from depend-
ence on Spain, James had cleared himself from all responsibility for the inevitable clash with the Spaniards and he
would, in addition, be provided with a perfect excuse
for ridding himself of the troublesome prisoner. This
policy of protection made it practically impossible for
Ralegh to succeed.

D

It took many months for plans to be made, funds raised and an expedition prepared. Few reliable men could be persuaded to entrust themselves on an enterprise so dubious. The seamen and soldiers Ralegh managed to collect, he later frankly called 'scum'—and their behaviour bears him out. Of the gentlemen, many were the black-sheep of families pleased to see the back of them. The total force consisted of 14 ships and pinnaces and about 1,000 men all told. Laurence Keymis and Ralegh's son, Walter, were among the leading officers. Ill-luck dogged the expedition from the time the fleet forgathered in the spring of 1617. The setbacks caused by contrary winds, disaffection and desertions, and crippling disease are almost unbelievable. When the fleet arrived off the South American coast in November after spending months on a voyage that should have taken weeks, Ralegh himself fell a victim to the fever which had ravaged his force. He lay dangerously ill for many days and when they reached the mouth of the Orinoco, he was unable to walk. It was impossible for him to lead in person the search for the gold-mine on the success of which his whole future depended.

There was no help for it: Ralegh sent off the five ships able to negotiate the river with 150 sailors and 250 soldiers. He put his nephew George Ralegh in charge of the land forces, since sickness and death had robbed him of his original commanders, and appointed Keymis as leader of the expedition. Keymis had served Ralegh with ardent loyalty, faith and affection over the years ever since he had left his Fellowship at Balliol to follow him. He had been with him in Guiana in 1595, had led a second expedition there in 1596, had accompanied him at the storming of Fayal, besides suffering the threat of the rack in 1603 when the case against his master was being prepared. For one who knew the territory, and who enthusiastically identified himself with Ralegh's aims, there could seem no better man, and his ensuing actions are all the more incomprehensible.

What actually happened in the Orinoco between 10 December, 1617 and 2 March, 1618 is obscure in the extreme. The new evidence brought to light by Professor V. T. Harlow and, more recently, by Miss A. M. C. Latham introduces new problems and perplexities. It almost seems that unless we can call back Keymis from the dead, the full story will never be known.

We do not know precisely where Ralegh and Keymis expected to find their gold-mine, nor where they expected to find the Spanish settlement of San Thomé. Modern investigators talk of *two* mines, Ralegh's intention being to work the one well inland from the river and nearer the sea than the other, though he had never seen it, nor, in all probability, had Keymis. But all the evidence seems to me to point to the place where Ralegh in 1595 had dug up gold-bearing ore a few miles south of the Orinoco where the river Caroni joins the main flood. In this region Keymis had found, on his return to Guiana in 1596, a Spanish settlement of 'some twenty or thirty houses'. There had been rumours that this garrison was moving to a new site, but clearly the mine was to be approached warily. Ralegh finally instructed Keymis to throw out the land force as a screen between the mine and the town, if they found the town near enough to be likely to cause trouble, while he went to open the mine. If the mine proved 'royal', then it did not matter so much about the Spaniards: if they attacked, then they were to be driven as far as might be.

In the event, after three weeks of toiling up the Orinoco, harassed by Spanish snipers from the banks, the company suddenly found themselves off San Thomé. Keymis later explained to Ralegh that they were taken by surprise because the settlement had been moved from where he had found it 20 years before; Ralegh repeated this statement in his *Apology*. Now, in fact, it has been proved that the settlement was substantially in the same place as before; Ralegh has been accused of lying in this matter of a removal. Certainly the distance of 20 miles he gives in his *Apology* is inexplicable, but I see no reason for discrediting his word entirely. The settlement *had* been rebuilt, and Keymis (in letters which have only just come to light) is most emphatic that there had been a removal. Even making allowances for his great anxiety to cover up his blunder of stumbling upon the town before he was aware of it, we must grant him that the San Thomé of 1617 was perhaps a mile or two away from where the San Thomé of 1596 had stood: a sufficient distance, in fact, to account for the present disaster.

Keymis hurriedly landed his men a few miles from the town and sent the larger boats up the river to size up the position. They were fired upon by the Spaniards. After some hours the English troops moved forward closer to the town, trying to make the best of the situation and invest the town without attacking it, in obedience to the spirit of Ralegh's orders. But they fell into a Spanish ambush. Out of the confusion that sprang up—it was now night—Ralegh's son, Walter, thinking more of glory than what was politic, closed with the enemy and, in the running fight that developed, fell mortally wounded. Once begun, the attack had to be maintained and the town was taken. The garrison, consisting only of 36 men, took to the woods with the inhabitants, leaving three dead behind them: the English lost three men besides Walter Ralegh.

A clash with the Spaniards and the loss of Ralegh's own son was an appalling start; and the Spanish threat was as great as ever even though San Thomé had fallen. From the beginning, Keymis was unable to take control of the situation. The troops were an unruly rabble and little could be done to induce the necessary order for the next stage of fortifying the settlement and preparing to open the mine. A week after the storming of the town Keymis had taken no step to achieve the object of the expedition, although in a letter he sent back to Ralegh to break to him the news of the death of his son, he spoke complacently of the many evidences of gold-working in the town and his intention to go straight to the mine, which he reckoned to be eight miles off. But a kind of paralysis seems to have seized him; now of all times, he realised he was not certain how to reach the mine through the thickly-wooded terrain from the town. He made one attempt, and brought back something that glistered but was not gold. He made unavailing efforts to find and operate the Spanish workings. Then, apparently in an effort to get to the mine from further up the river, he led an expedition out by boat. Quite incomprehensibly, he went past the mouth of the Caroni and the party fell into a Spanish ambush, eight of them being killed or wounded. Even less explicable was his next step; he took three boats a hundred miles and more up the Orinoco, sounding all the way, pretending to be searching for a passage to the mine, until the shallows stopped their passage. He never told Ralegh how far he went, though he was away three weeks, but simply claimed he was trying to overcome the insuperable difficulty of getting to the shore with very little water in the river.

Keymis was in a desperate position. He could not

or would not make a determined effort to get to the Caroni mine. No-one trusted him. The handful of Spaniards kept the English in a nightmare of fear with their successful guerrilla raids, 250 of the original 400 men had been lost, and the morale of the remainder was at rock-bottom. Keymis could not keep the force in San Thomé whether he wanted to or not. The troops set the town ablaze and there was nothing for it but to set sail down the Orinoco.

At Trinidad Ralegh was waiting. He had heard from Keymis of the death of his son, and Indians had brought rumours of the fighting in the town. On 2 March, the expedition returned and Ralegh learned the whole horrifying truth: that there was no gold and that nothing had been achieved save the burning of a Spanish settlement. His stupefaction and anger may easily be imagined. Keymis justified himself with a multiplicity of excuses for not having opened the mine: Ralegh utterly rejected them all, told him he had ruined him for ever and that he would hold him responsible to the King for the failure of the expedition. Keymis came again to him with a letter of explanation to Lord Arundel: Ralegh persisted in refusing to take his part. 'I know then, Sir, what course to take,' answered Keymis, and left Ralegh's cabin for his own. A moment later a shot was heard; Ralegh sent up (in his own words) 'to know who shot the pistol: Keymis himself made answer, lying on his bed, that he had shot it off because it had been long charged, with which I was satisfied. Some half an hour after this, his boy, going in to his cabin, found him dead, having a long knife thrust under his left pap through his heart, and the pistol lying by him, with which it appeared he had shot himself, but the bullet, lighting upon a rib, had but broken the rib, and went no further.'

The suicide of the wretched Keymis did not lessen Ralegh's anger against him: he considered the act a confession of guilt. Ralegh's behaviour is painful, but we can no longer apply to him the standards we should apply to a man entirely in his right mind. The loss of his son, the utter failure of the expedition, the grim prospect of what awaited him in England, laid on him a greater weight than he could bear. He conceived the frenzied notion of leading an expedition back again up the river. It was a vain proposition: he could not have forced the sullen and discontented men a mile on the journey. He hoisted sail and turned his back on Guiana, the 'rich and beautiful empire' and grave of all his hopes. The fleet began to break up, two captains deserting to privateer on their own account. Ralegh wrote to one who had been his friend at home, Secretary Winwood, not knowing he had died months before:

> What shall become of me now, I know not; I am unpardoned in England, and my poor estate consumed, and whether any other Prince or State will give me bread, I know not. I desire your Honour to hold me in your good opinion, and to remember my service to my lords of Arundel and Pembroke; to take some pity on my poor wife, to whom I dare not write, for the renewing of her sorrows for her son. And I beseech you to give a copy of these to my Lord Carew; for to a broken mind, to a weak body and weak eyes, it is a torment to write many letters.

Then he summoned his spirits to compose the letter he had thought he dared not write to his wife: ' . . . Comfort your heart, dear Bess; I shall sorrow for us both, and I shall sorrow the less because I have not long to sorrow, because not long to live . . . The Lord bless you and comfort you, that you may bear patiently the death of your valiant son.'

The Return

Whatever course may have suggested itself to Ralegh,
of fleeing to France, of privateering, the fact is that he
sailed home. The rest of his fleet deserted, and he was
left alone. He resisted the suggestions of his own crew
that he should turn pirate; they mutinied and he still
resisted. Finally he came to terms with them and agreed
to land the mutineers in Ireland. Then he made the
best of his way to Plymouth. As he came into harbour,
he sat down to write to Lord Carew; for he had heard
something of the reception that awaited him:

> . . . at the manifest peril of my life I have brought myself
> and my ship to England. I have suffered as many miseries as
> it was possible for me to suffer, which I could not have
> endured if God had not given me strength. If His Majesty
> wishes that I should suffer even more, let God's will be
> done . . .

It is quite clear that Ralegh had not fully realised that it
was against the attack on and destruction of San Thomé
that the King's displeasure was to be directed. All the
letters written before he touched at Ireland give long
explanations of the failure to reach the mine; the taking
of the town, though he deplores it, he dismisses as an
unavoidable act forced on the English by Spanish aggression. He had even commended to the King the services
of those who had distinguished themselves in the action!
Even now, when he is 'alarmed not a little' to hear that
James is pronouncing his deep anger at the collision, he
is bewildered also: 'though I gave no authority for it,
it was impossible to avoid!' he expostulates. Patently,
Ralegh did not understand his sovereign's mind. The
fact that James had allowed him to go, he had all along
interpreted as meaning that, whatever might be told to

the Spanish Ambassador, the King accepted Ralegh's doctrine that Guiana was English, and was prepared to risk a clash with the Spanish outposts. In all his self-justifications from this point, Ralegh harps on this theme: if James did not accept Ralegh's claim that Guiana was rightfully English territory, why did he let him go at all? And how could Spanish atrocities against the English be forgotten while an English defence against a Spanish attack was called a murderous act? But James was not prepared to accept the consequences of risks inherent in an enterprise he had permitted. He was now reaping the harvest of his own unwisdom in wishing to get the best of both worlds. The negotiations for the Spanish marriage between Charles and the Infanta stood at a delicate balance; Ralegh's actions and empty-handed return placed him in a predicament he could have entirely avoided. Even before Ralegh had landed, the King published his 'utter mislike and detestation' of 'the insolences and excesses' which 'common fame' reported to have been committed by Ralegh against the territories and subjects of his 'dear brother the King of Spain'. He did put up a weak resistance to Gondomar's vengeful demands, but succumbed on the day after Ralegh's arrival at Plymouth and agreed that Ralegh should be handed over to the King of Spain to be hanged out of hand in Madrid. As it turned out, King Philip was quite ready to leave the office of providing a scaffold and an executioner to his dear brother of England.

Ralegh was met by his wife, and, with the faithful Captain King, made preparations to set out for London. His kinsman Sir Lewis Stukeley was sent by the Government to escort him. It may seem madness to us that Ralegh returned to England, and it certainly seemed madness to his wife and Samuel King. The surveillance was lax, and at last Ralegh was persuaded to flee to France. But hardly had the boat put off towards the waiting ship than Ralegh's determination to face his accusers returned, and he made the boat put back. With Stukeley and a horrible French doctor, Manourie, acting as a spy on Ralegh, the party set off towards London. At Salisbury, Ralegh feigned an illness to gain time to write his *Apology*, and perhaps to gain a chance of an audience with James, who was on progress in the vicinity. The *Apology* for the failure of the Guiana expedition, Ralegh's full justification of his policies and behaviour, is a mixed work, and bears the whole stamp of the mental strain under which he was labouring. Unanswerable logic lies side by side with a querulous rationalising of his actions; quiet bitterness accompanies hectic pleading; righteous indignation sometimes gives way to something more histrionic as he complains of his own afflictions and undeserved sufferings. The usefulness of the work as a factual account of the voyage is marred by the exigencies of Ralegh's situation when he wrote it, and his urgent desire to clear himself. Historians have been baffled by contradictions and have called Ralegh's truthfulness to account; yet everyone of us puts his own past actions and motives in the light most favourable to himself, and few of us have had such pressing need to justify ourselves as Ralegh had. Yet as the 'illness' abated and the party moved on again to London, Ralegh must have realised the futility of defending himself. He had written that 'as good success admits of no examination of errors, so the contrary allows of no excuse how reasonable or just soever'.

In London in early August Ralegh had seen and heard enough to convince him that there was little hope for him; at last he resolved to fly. French agents had been in touch with him all the way, and plans were made for an escape to France in a ketch. Stukeley, who had been professing all these weeks his concern for Ralegh's interests, was enrolled in the party. Boats were hired and at night the group set off down the Thames to join the ketch. It was a cat-and-mouse game: the owner of the ketch and the agent who procured it—the one formerly in King's service, the other in Ralegh's—betrayed the plans to the Government for cash. Stukeley was waiting only for a dramatic moment to reveal his patriotic zeal and his true colours—satanic ones. The boats were followed, and at the right moment Ralegh was arrested in the King's name; the next morning he was in the Tower. The reader may pass his own judgment on Ralegh for choosing to flee, but he must admit that there is something remarkable in a man who for so long since his release had refused to play Coriolanus to a King and country that had so monstrously wronged him. All along he looked steadily and with courage at those who accused and maligned him, and only turned aside when he realised that, for a second time, justice would under no circumstances be granted to him.

With Ralegh in the Tower, the government began in earnest to build up a case against him. Sir Thomas Wilson was put with him as a supposed friend, to try to extort confessions—but there was nothing to be gained there. Those who wish for arguments in support of the accusations piled up against Ralegh in the autumn of 1618 may turn to S. R. Gardiner's article in *The Fortnightly Review* for 1867. The government held that the mine was a fiction, and the professed purpose of the expedition a hoax invented by Ralegh to gain his freedom; that Ralegh held a privateering commission from the French and that he had intended to prey upon the Spanish Plate Fleet; and, of course, that he had committed a flagrant breach of international peace in attacking a Spanish settlement, breaking his vow to the King into the bargain.

There was much discussion on how Ralegh should be finally arraigned. The King was told that, since the prisoner was still unpardoned for the capital treason of 1603, he could legally be executed without further trial; in any case, he could not be tried for a crime committed since an attainder for treason. The Commissioners of the case recommended a course, 'nearest to a legal procedure', of bringing Ralegh before the Council and an audience of observers, charging him and hearing his defence. As it was, James chose to have the Commissioners only, without observers: an asinine procedure that gave the public the impression that Ralegh was being condemned in hugger-mugger, without any real fault, as a sacrifice to Spain in the interests of forwarding the unpopular Spanish Marriage.

Before this tribunal on 22 October, Ralegh repudiated the charges against him along the lines of his *Apology*. But his defence was given scant respect. On 23 October, he was told that he was to be executed for his crime of 1603. In vain was Ralegh's life pleaded for by his remaining son and by the Queen herself. Ralegh disdained to plead himself, once the sentence had been confirmed. The Dean of Westminster, appointed to attend him, reported of him as he awaited the fulfilment of the sentence: 'He was the most fearless of death that ever was known; and the most resolute and confident, yet with reverence and conscience.'

Ralegh was executed on the morning of 29 October, 1618, in Old Palace Yard at Westminster. A large crowd had assembled, and friends and enemies of rank were there to witness his end. He bore himself with complete dignity and self-possession. 'In all the time he was on the scaffold, nor before, there appeared not the least alteration in his voice or countenance,' wrote an observer, 'but he seemed as free from all manner of apprehension, as if he had been come hither rather to be a spectator than a sufferer; nay, the beholders seemed much more sensible than did he.' After greeting his friends, he spoke —for three-quarters of an hour, it is said; we have only imperfect reports of his speech. 'I thank my God heartily that he hath brought me into the light to die, and hath not suffered me to die in the dark prison of the Tower where I have suffered a great deal of adversity and a long sickness.' He defended himself against disloyalty to the King ('But in this I speak now, what have I to do with kings? I have nothing to do with them: I have now to do with God'), he warned his hearers against the duplicity of Sir Lewis Stukeley, he rejected the accusations that there had been no mine, and no intention of returning to England. Finally he spoke of Essex, and denied that he had engineered his death or insulted him at his execution.

Then he made himself ready for death. He asked to see the axe: 'Dost thou think that I am afraid of it?' He felt its edge and said with a smile, 'This is that that will cure all sorrows.' He would not be blindfolded, nor did he care which way he faced: 'So the heart be right, it is no matter which way the head lies.' He granted the executioner's request for forgiveness and placed himself at the block. There being a pause, he called out to the headsman 'asking him why he did not strike. "Strike, man!" said he; and so, in two blows, was delivered from his pain.'

Chapter Two

THE RENAISSANCE IMAGINATION

WE have grown rather shy of using the term 'Renaissance': as we know more, it becomes increasingly hard to say *when* it was or *what* it was. I use the word to define that long period of overlap between the medieval and the modern worlds: a period for which the thirteenth century is hardly too early a beginning or the eighteenth too late a close, when new values, our values, began to contest the old; a period whose commonest quality is tension, in which two ages, one dying and one being born, strive for mastery. The tension is in religion, philosophy, morals, politics, economic and social structure. The peculiar vigour that we recognise in the period in both literature and action derives, perhaps, from this very tension: a safe sleep is impossible when all assumptions and traditions are challenged; either the old ways must be explained and defended or the new ways must be fought for. The period in England when the tension between old and new is at its peak, and most stirred men's minds, is of course, the late Elizabethan and the Stuart period; Shakespeare's tragedies, the growth of nonconformity, *The Advancement of Learning*, the colonising of America, the Civil War and *Paradise Lost*, are all witnesses of the clash of meeting currents.

It is hard to think of any one person who better embodies the various elements, the conflicts and contradictions of old beliefs and new attitudes, who better sums

46

up in himself the inimitable imagination of this period of stress that we call the Renaissance in England, than Sir Walter Ralegh. He is the ideal Renaissance case-history.

The Compleat Gentleman

His very versatility points to the ideal of the age that the courtier or 'compleat gentleman' should strive to fulfil all the functions open to a man, should live with the whole of his being and not just a part of it. It was not enough for a man to be a statesman, or a poet, or an expert in the history of his country, or a soldier; he must try to unite the practical, the active, the artistic, the intellectual ways of living within his own life. In his *Mother Hubberds Tale* Spenser describes the perfect courtier (to fashion whom, he wrote his *Faerie Queene*), who desires to serve his Prince with honour, and can do so

> Whether for armes and warlike amenaunce
> Or else for wise and civill governaunce,

who delights as much in exercising his body as feeding his mind or entertaining himself with music; one for whom there is no greater pleasure than

> wise discourse
> Of Natures workes, of heavens continuall course,
> Of forreine lands, of people different,
> Of kingdomes change, of divers gouvernment.

That the ideal was more than mere talk is obvious if one thinks of men like Sir Philip Sidney, a pattern of Christian behaviour, a highly skilled poet and critic, interested in the new science, and an example of service to his country in peace and war. That Ralegh was considerably less than a model of Christian behaviour and that he was never officially a statesman, goes without saying. But by his capacity for excellence in so very many spheres, as courtier, soldier, historian, poet, scientist, explorer, administrator, he too is a living example of the belief of his age that a man should develop all his potentialities and realise his whole personality.

He was, first, very closely identified with the intellectual life of his times: he sought knowledge as zealously as he sought position and honour. It was, of course, much easier in his day for a man whose life was largely spent in business and active matters to acquire a real proficiency in all branches of learning because the extent of human knowledge was so much smaller than it is now. Nevertheless, supreme energy was needed to become more than a mere dabbler in the various arts and sciences, and that Ralegh had this energy is clear from the early accounts. 'He was an indefatigable reader, whether by sea or land', said Naunton, and David Lloyd tells us that 'five hours he slept, four he read, two he discoursed, allowing the rest to his business and necessities. . . . So contemplative he was, that you would think he was not active: so active that you would say he was not prudent—a great soldier, and yet an excellent courtier; an accomplished gallant and yet a bookish man.' At his trial, when questioned about his possession of a suspicious writing, by one Snagge, which Cobham had borrowed from his library, he protested that there was no book published in those days, when he was a young man, that he did not buy. In the Tower, he took more true comfort in those prison-companions, his books, 'than ever he took of his courtly companions in his chiefest bravery', according to Sir John Harrington.[1]

[1] In the extremely interesting notebook recently identified as Ralegh's by Mr. W. F. Oakeshott (see *The Times*, 29 November 1952, and below, pp. 101 and 147), Ralegh has set about making a catalogue of books. They may well be those he had with him in the Tower; most of them would be useful to an

Interest in the past was one of the significant intellectual developments of the Renaissance; it is associated
with the growth both of science and of nationalism—
science, in the sense that man begins to be curious about
himself, sees himself as an object for empirical study
and begins to question his own development from early
times; nationalism, in the sense that a people's awareness
of themselves as a nation made them inquisitive about
their background. There will be much to say in a later
chapter of Ralegh's efforts as an historian. His *History
of the World* is one of the major achievements of his life.
He gave years to the work, and the patience and pains
and thought expended in tackling the many formidable
difficulties are not to be made light of. In its time, his
History was a great and original contribution to the study
of man and it still expounds, to an age which has out-
grown Ralegh's methods of research, an important philosophy and outlook on life. That this philosophy is largely
a medieval philosophy at once reminds us of the strange
blending of the old and the new in this typical Renaissance man.

The new spirit of scientific historical enquiry found
expression in England in the formation of the Society of
Antiquaries, probably about the year 1580. All too little
is known about the Society, but the seriousness of the
group can be measured by the terms of their application
to the Queen to become formally incorporated as a royal
historical society, with a library; this society and library
would have a national responsibility for collecting and
preserving records and matters of general historical
interest. It is not certain whether Ralegh was an official

historian. The general books range from 'A treatis of specters' to 'Opera
Petrarchæ', 'Cassanion de gigantibus' to 'Essays French', 'Laurentius præser-
vation of health' to 'Cardanus de subtilitate'; Copernicus, Machiavelli, Pico
della Mirandola, Hakluyt and Camden are represented.

member of this very select group, but he was closely
associated with several of its fellows (who included
Camden, Lancelot Andrewes, Lambard and Stowe).
There exists an interesting letter of Ralegh's, written
from the Tower to Sir Robert Cotton, a guiding spirit
of the society, giving a list of books and manuscripts relating to British antiquities that Ralegh wished to borrow.
John Hooker and Richard Carew were other antiquaries
with whom Ralegh was in intimate association.

Ralegh's close connexions with the scientific move-
ments of his day are extremely important, but as they
bring up the whole general problem of his intellectual
attitude, they must be left for later discussion.

Ralegh's preoccupation with the world of learning
can be seen in the delight he had in being surrounded by
scholars. His patronage of the mathematician Thomas
Harriot brings him as much credit, almost, as anything
else in his life. His lieutenant and assistant, Keymis, had
been a Fellow of Balliol; his interests extended from the
writing of Latin verse to geography and mathematics.
One John Talbot shared Ralegh's imprisonment for eleven
years and went on the last Guiana expedition with him,
to win only a brief epitaph that Ralegh scribbled in his
journal: ' . . . my honest friend, an excellent general
scholar, and as faithful and true man as lived'.

Turning now to Ralegh's interest in the arts, we find
that here he is indeed at the centre of the life of his time.
Music and painting he encouraged with his purse, and in
poetry there is the wealth that it is a chief part of this
book's purpose to discuss. Ralegh was deservedly one of
the most admired of the court-poets and, as we should
expect, he was in some way associated with three of the
four major poets of his time, Spenser, Marlowe and
Jonson, as well as lesser figures from an earlier period,

like Gascoigne and Churchyard. Ralegh's associations with Shakespeare have naturally been explored by some who have been determined that the exploration should not be unfruitful: but there is no real evidence of any association.

Marlowe hovers most tantalizingly on the fringes of the Ralegh circle. In the charges of atheism brought against him there are indications of some slight relationship between the dramatist and the courtier, but much better, if impressionistic evidence, seems to lie in the *mood* of Ralegh's 'Answer' to Marlowe's 'Come Live With Me and Be My Love': if this gentle ridicule of a poem never meant seriously in the first place is not a game between two friends, it is difficult to know what it is. Ralegh's relations with Spenser were intimate and details are embedded in Spenser's verse: the next chapter discusses them. Jonson's references to Ralegh are not glowing, but he was on friendly enough terms to lend him assistance with the *History of the World*. Mention of Jonson brings up the vexed question of the 'Mermaid Club': it would be very rash to enter into the debate on how much fact lies behind the legends of the meetings of wits and poets at the Mermaid Tavern. Aubrey talks of Ralegh's being a member of a 'sodality' of 'heroes and wits' which met at the 'Mermaid in Friday Street', but it is not very likely that Ralegh did much tavern-hunting after his youth. The sessions of the poets at the Mermaid about which Beaumont wrote to Jonson—'What things we have seen done at the Mermaid!'—can refer only to a time after Ralegh had been imprisoned.

Ralegh's most important poetic fellowships were with those gifted amateurs at court whose work so enriches Elizabethan literature. In Henry VIII's reign, Wyatt and Surrey had set a high standard for court poetry. George

Puttenham, in his *Art of English Poesie*, described their successors:

> And in Her Majesty's time that now is, are sprung up another crew of courtly makers, noblemen and gentlemen of Her Majesty's own servants, who have written excellently well, as it would appear if their doings could be found out and made public with the rest, of which number is first that noble gentleman, Edward, Earl of Oxford, Thomas, Lord of Buckhurst (when he was young), Henry Lord Paget, Sir Philip Sidney, Sir Walter Ralegh, Master Edward Dyer, Master Fulke Greville, Gascoigne, Breton, Turberville and a great many other learned gentlemen, whose names I do not omit for envy, but to avoid tediousness, and who have deserved no little commendation.

These courtly poets, as Puttenham's words indicate, gave little thought to publishing their works. Their poems were not written for unknown men who bought books and read them in their scattered homes. They wrote for their own circle in court; poems were passed round in manuscript and then thought of no more. Written for particular occasions and for a particular group, written without an eye to fame among a wide public or among after-generations, this verse is yet often the freshest and finest of the age. Like the popular dramatist, the courtier-poet effaced himself as a personality and took no particular care to prolong the life of his art. Though this attitude is in many ways admirable, it has left a heritage of problems to the modern scholar. Much court-poetry has not survived, and the authorship of what has been (almost by accident) preserved is often very uncertain. A typical perplexity is the difficulty of disentangling the poems of Sir Arthur Gorges (Ralegh's close friend and captain of his flagship in the Islands Voyage) from Ralegh's own.

The extent of Ralegh's verse-writing is very difficult to assess. Much that he wrote has been lost, and no-one can say how much, or whether what we have represents his best work. At every turn there is the problem of authorship: poems which are indisputably Ralegh's are very scarce; works are given to him on the slender evidence of initials in printed anthologies or ascriptions in manuscript collections and commonplace books—or on the dangerous logic of style. There is hardly a poem where the true text can be confidently established: most poems appear in widely different versions in different manuscripts. (Luckily, we have the long poem of *The Ocean to Cynthia* in Ralegh's own handwriting, and here these problems do not arise.)

Aubrey held that Ralegh 'was sometimes a poet: not often', but the sureness of style and discipline of craftsmanship in the majority of poems which are fairly certainly his would seem to argue that Ralegh was very much more than an occasional versifier. Miss Latham well says that to a man like Ralegh, poetry was 'as natural as breathing'; his first poem which can be dated was written when he was twenty-four, and on the night before his death (so goes the tradition) he composed his own epitaph in verse: all his life, Ralegh was a poet. He was not, of course, a poet in the dedicated sense like the English Romantics, nor was he a man for whom poetry was the only means of expressing his imagination; he was a poet because his age encouraged him, as a courtier and gentleman, to write verse, because the circles in which he moved provided an attentive audience with sensibility like his own, and because his own genius continually found occasions needing the comment of poetry, which his talents could most ably supply.

If, to these wide interests of Ralegh, we add his achievements in so many directions in the world of action, we see how his versatility not only reflects the Renaissance ideal of courtly behaviour, but shows how he shares the life of his age in all its variety.

The Spirit of the Age

It remains to look at Ralegh as the embodiment of his age at deeper levels of the spirit. We may well begin with his intense and individualistic ambition, which is a Renaissance theme if there ever was one. The modern American belief in the virtue and necessity of 'getting to the top' has as its illustrious ancestor the spirit that drove those Elizabethans who were not born to great place and wealth to exercise their whole beings in the colourful attainment of them. Tamburlaine the Great may or may not have been an object of admiration to the Elizabethans, but, as Marlowe presents him, he is certainly the incarnation of an Elizabethan spirit of self-assertion, which the modern world must also recognise as its own. Ralegh possessed this spirit of self-assertion to the full; in a way, his whole life is a record of striving for money, position and power for himself. But immediately we find the Renaissance paradox. *The History of the World* is unceasing in its condemnation of personal ambition, that 'eldest and most monstrous vice', synonymous with Pride, the first of the seven deadly sins. Ralegh's attitude to the struggle of nations shows exactly the same paradox as his attitude to the struggle of individuals: in his writings, he condemns the strife of nations for mastery as mere viciousness and greed, yet in his life he is an ardent nationalist, believing wholeheartedly in the greatness of his nation and the need for England to exalt herself among other nations by crushing her rivals, particularly Spain.

This paradox between words and deeds shows lack of logic and consistency, but no more hypocrisy than the age itself must answer for. For the notion that the un-principled struggle for power in both nations and indi-viduals was evil, was something the age inherited from the Middle Ages and was very deeply embedded in its thinking. But the world of ideas was lagging behind the world of action. The static medieval age was over; 'progress' had begun, and progress demanded self-assertion. Ralegh seems unaware of the discrepancy between the two ideals, but he reflects the tension of his age in sanctioning in his active career the ambition which he denounced as selfishness and self-aggrandisement when he reflected on it *sub specie aeternatis*.

The age's paradoxes and ambiguities are reflected very clearly in Ralegh's colonial ambitions. What was he trying to achieve? What spirit led him on? There are a dozen answers, cynical or romantic in varying degrees, all perhaps partly true and no one wholly true. Ralegh was out for personal profit and power; he was the instru-ment of the laws of economic development, ushering in the period of imperialist expansion; he was a symbol of the awakening mind of man, seeking to explore the globe and extend mastery over nature; he was a conscious exponent of nationalism; he was the embodiment of the Elizabethan spirit of adventure. Ralegh himself, as he wrote his *History of the World*, was often perplexed to account for the leading motives of men in bringing about some important action. Had he understood how subtle and tangled his own motives were, and of necessity were, as the spear-head of Elizabethan imperialism, he might have worried less about choosing a single, dominant motive inspiring the behaviour of others.

Atheism and Science

Ralegh's religious views were in his own day, and have
remained ever since, the subject of a babel of ill-founded
gossip. His 'atheism' was as much a matter of course as
his pride, in popular judgment. The jesuit controver-
sialist, Robert Parsons, made in 1592 the famous attack
on Sir Walter Ralegh's 'School of Atheism', 'wherein
both Moses and Our Saviour, the Old and New Testament
are jested at, and the scholars taught among other things
to spell God backward.' In 1594, a commission which
met at Cerne Abbas to investigate allegations of godlessness and heretical opinions in Dorset heard alarming
stories about Ralegh. The Rev. Nicholas Jeffries had
'heard by report of divers that Sir Walter Ralegh and his
retinue are generally suspected of atheism' and had also
heard that Harriot had been before the Lords of the
Council for denying the resurrection of the body. The
minister of Gillingham could not remember who told
him, but he had heard that Ralegh's man Harriot had
brought the Godhead into question. The curate of
Motcombe knew the general report that Ralegh could
reason against the omnipotence of God. The Reverend
Ralph Ironside had a longer tale to tell, and, what is
more, a tale not based on hearsay, but his evidence must
be considered later. In 1603, at his trial, Ralegh was a
'damnable atheist' to Coke, and Popham would not
repeat the 'heathenish, blasphemous, atheistical and
profane opinions' which the world taxed Ralegh with
holding and which Christian ears could not endure to hear.

Well after Ralegh's death, the 'scandal of atheism'
still clung to his name. Aubrey had heard the stories, and
had come to the conclusion that, rather than an atheist,
Ralegh was a non-Christian Deist—a position taught to

him by Harriot. In the present century, a new and ingenious story has emerged: the story of the 'School of Night'. According to this, the School of Atheism was a society of satanists, including literary figures, Marlowe, Chapman and Roydon; noblemen, the Earls of Derby and Northumberland; scholars, Harriot, Keymis and Walter Warner. This esoteric society dedicated itself to the arcane and occult in art and science, and its members were distinguished for holding in common very 'advanced' and 'progressive' views on religion and politics. Opposed to it was a group owing allegiance to Essex and Southampton, the spokesman of which was Shakespeare, whose *Love's Labour's Lost* was the group's manifesto and an attack on Ralegh's society. Much has been written about this society,[1] but I have never been persuaded that the 'School of Night' ever existed in reality; the evidence adduced to support the theory has to my mind been convincingly discredited by two American scholars, P. H. Kocher and E. A. Strathmann.[2]

Professor Strathmann has, indeed, earned the gratitude of all interested in Ralegh and the Elizabethan intellectual climate for his very patient and thorough examination of Ralegh's religious views. He is able to show that, however the pregnant and versatile term 'atheist' might have been intended to apply to Ralegh, his expressed opinions everywhere clear him of the charge. Sometimes, of course, 'atheist' is simply used as a term of abuse. Parsons' charges are shown to be part of a Catholic campaign to discredit Elizabeth's counsellors and favourites and to have no value as evidence. If Ralegh *had* been an atheist or a violent heretic or a Deist or a pagan or an

---

[1] e.g. M. C. Bradbrook, *The School of Night* (1936).

[2] *Christopher Marlowe* (1946), pp. 7–18; *Sir Walter Ralegh: A Study of Elizabethan Scepticism* (1951), pp. 262–271.

agnostic, the whole argument of this chapter would crumble, for he would cease to represent his very religious and orthodox age. But no-one who has paid careful attention to Ralegh's own words can have doubt that he was a sincere and fundamentally orthodox Christian.

It is easy enough to see why Ralegh and orthodox religious feeling have never seemed to go together. He was associated with the *avant-garde* of the scientific movement which eventually broke down the medieval Christian attitude of mind and, secondly, his haughtiness of manner, determination to question things, lack of restraint in expressing his opinions, would often obscure from his contemporaries his genuine and profound piety. Let us look at some of the cross-currents in Ralegh's faith, and first, his connexions with science.

Science was still a suspect occupation in Ralegh's day—an impious prying into the secrets of Creation, an arrogant presumption and a seeking for a power that God did not intend man to have. Chapter Eleven of the first book of Ralegh's *History of the World* contains a very interesting and spirited defence of 'lawful magic'; it makes a separation of that knowledge of the secrets of nature which can be considered not only legitimate but laudable, from the black and devilish arts of the Faustian kind: a defence, in fact, of the fundamental piety of proper scientific investigation. 'The third kind of magic,' he says, for example, 'containeth the whole philosophy of nature; not the brabblings of the Aristotelians, but that which bringeth to light the inmost virtues and draweth them out of nature's hidden bosom to human use.' God had given hidden properties to His Creation, and it is a right and necessary endeavour of man to investigate these virtues and apply them for 'the help and comfort of mankind'.

This justification of science as a means of ministering to the needs of mankind is characteristic of the age, and is reminiscent of Francis Bacon's approach. Actually, science was identified in the sixteenth century with practical needs: 'pure' investigation was not very interesting to a man like Ralegh. The union of mathematics and astronomy with the practical needs of navigation is a classic example of how knowledge and its application went hand in hand. John Dee and Thomas Harriot were the greatest of the sixteenth-century scientists in England, and with both of them Ralegh associated for the main purpose of aiding discovery and exploration. Ralegh (and others like him) financed and encouraged these men; the work they did in solving the kind of problems he set them really marks the beginning of the co-operative scientific activity in England that culminated in the founding of the Royal Society at the Restoration. Dee was a sort of Royal Society himself, in a way; he had immense influence, and his work as technical adviser to all the great Elizabethan explorers makes a fascinating story. All sorts of problems, the compass, cartography, ascertaining latitude and longitude, needed the help of his mathematical and astronomical knowledge, and he freely dispensed his aid to Frobisher, Drake, Gilbert, and Ralegh. Hakluyt was one who learned from Dee, and he very clearly recognises the association of research with practical needs in his dedication to Ralegh of Peter Martyr's *Decades of the New World* (1587):

> Since you clearly saw that skill in the arts of navigation, the chief glory of an insular nation, would obtain its greatest splendour among us by the firm support of the mathematical sciences, you have trained up and supported now a long time, with a most liberal salary, Thomas Harriot, a young man well versed in those studies, in order that you

might acquire in your spare hours by his instruction a knowledge of those noble sciences, and your own numerous sea-captains might unite profitable theory with practice.

Harriot worked with Ralegh in many capacities over a number of years. He was sent to Virginia, and he returned with a very fine account of the country (printed in Hakluyt), his survey ranging from Indian religious customs to the potentialities for agriculture. It is important to understand just what care Ralegh took, as in this instance, to make sure that all his expeditions should be fully scientific explorations. With the men and means at his disposal, he had as much concern in this matter as the organisers of a modern polar expedition have. His own *Discovery of Guiana* is spoken of highly as a 'geographical classic' by the great authority on Tudor geography, Professor E. G. R. Taylor. We have to remember that men whose heads grow beneath their shoulders are but one mistaken report in an account that shows Ralegh's great interest in and capacity for studying 'human' and physical geography. As in *The History of the World*, we cannot fail to be aware of Ralegh's absorption in the awakening sciences of man: in, for example, what we should call ethnography, anthropology and comparative religion.

Shipbuilding may seem a far cry from astronomy, but there is no drawing a hard and fast line between where research ended and its application to voyages of discovery began. A grateful sea-captain named some north-western islands 'Brigges His Mathematickes' after the Professor of Geometry at Gresham College. It has been recognized that in the early seventeenth century there was a close association between the mathematical professors of that nursery of English science, Gresham College, and the sea-captains and shipbuilders of the English navy. It is only reasonable to suppose that the building of ships engaged the minds of men of science at the end of the sixteenth century also. At any rate, Ralegh was noted for his experiments and innovations in shipbuilding, and for the money he spent on them. The *Bark Ralegh*, the *Ark Ralegh* (sold to the Crown in 1592) and the *Roebuck* were famous ships, and Howard, who used the *Ark Ralegh* as his flagship against the Armada called it 'the oddest ship in the world, and the best for all conditions'.

The Elizabethan world of science was, of course, a muddled and motley world. John Dee, one of the very few men to understand the real significance of the Copernican system, whose technical advances with Harriot and Digges in the use of the telescope anticipated the work of more famous continental scientists like Galileo, was yet a dabbler in occult sciences. It was his skill in alchemy and astrology as much as his more sober erudition that brought him to the notice of the Queen. He associated with the notorious mountebank and gaol-bird Edmund Kelly for the purpose of raising spirits, and a magic mirror of his, used for sorcery, is still preserved. Ironically, a mob which, infuriated by Dee's blasphemous indulgence in black magic, broke into his house in Mortlake, destroyed many of the really important and valuable scientific instruments and papers. An understanding of how thin the partitions were between the medieval world of magic and the modern world of inductive science helps us to appreciate Ralegh's 'aberrations': his exercises, for example, in homeopathic magic, which is really the only description of his 'sympathetic medicines' and his 'grand Cordial'.

There is no doubt at all that the scientific spirit, which Ralegh certainly shared, proved in the long run incompatible with the Christian modes of thought that inspired St. Augustine and Dante. The expense of time in measuring the phenomena of the visible world seemed a profitless activity to men who considered the purpose of existence to be the union of the soul with its creator. For Dante, it was fulfilment enough to come to the vision of one simple flame, the gathering of all the scattered leaves of the universe into one volume by the power of love, the love that moves the sun and the other stars. Modern scientific man seeks a different kind of knowledge from medieval religious man, and seeks it by different means. He seeks to know, not God, but the material world, in order that he may have power over the material world; faith, conscience and reason are not his instruments, but observation and experiment. There is a fundamental disagreement of attitude here; there was another disagreement which seems more superficial, but it was almost more important because more obvious: the fact that the results of the new scientific enquiry often seemed to deny the account of the world and human history given in the Bible.

Francis Bacon is perfectly aware that the new directions he wishes human thought to take are incompatible with traditional religious thought, and God holds an equivocal place in *The Advancement of Learning*; Bacon is not very much interested in knowledge that cannot be proved by experiment and put to the use of relieving man's physical estate. Sir Thomas Browne, on the other hand, is passionately concerned to preserve belief, and struggles hard to reconcile what are often, for him, the opposed teachings of faith and scientific enquiry. In Ralegh's work it is remarkable not to find either Bacon's avoidance or Browne's reconciliation. The core of his belief, which is that of the medieval Christian, is most surprisingly free from the kind of questionings and conflicts that one would have expected in one who did enthusiastically foster the new science. It is not stupidity or intellectual short-sightedness that produces this effect. Ralegh knows he has to make a choice, and traditional thinking is what he chooses. His religious faith is primary with him: God and the word of God are for him mightier things than the questionings of the human mind. Scientific knowledge may be used, as it is in *The History of the World*, to provide confirmation of the truth of the miracles and mysteries of the Christian faith; where human knowledge provides disturbingly different answers from those taught in the Bible and by the Church, it must be rejected, since it is arrogance for man to pit his petty mind against the received word of God. Ralegh does not reject scientific enquiry out of hand any more than he blindly and unquestioningly accepts his faith, but the point that must be made here is that his acquaintance with science has convinced him of the limitations of human knowledge; has taught him not arrogance, but humility. He turns to accept as fundamental a knowledge which he considers to derive from a higher source than the enquiries of the human mind.

Even so, Ralegh had too energetic a mind simply to take things on trust; he was determined to work things out for himself—always within the central beliefs. Sir John Harrington was among the few of Ralegh's contemporaries who could recognise that he was an independent thinker without being a revolutionary in religion. Just before Ralegh's trial he wrote: 'I wist not that he hath evil design in point of faith or religion. As he hath oft discoursed to me with much learning, wisdom and freedom, I know he doth somewhat differ in opinion from some others; but I think also his heart is well fixed in every honest thing, as far as I can look into him.'

For example, Ralegh was at one with Bacon in his contempt for the dogmatic utterances of Aristotle and the 'schoolmen'—the medieval fathers—and the awe and reverence commonly given to these utterances as the voice of traditional authority. Where these utterances concern matters of 'nature and finite power', that is to say the material world, the field open to scientific enquiry, Ralegh sturdily refuses to believe that the Ancients had better equipment for pronouncing truth than the moderns. 'I shall never be persuaded that God hath shut up all light of learning within the lanthorn of Aristotle's brains.' He demands freedom of intellectual inquiry into the nature of the physical world. Where these utterances, on the other hand, concern matters properly above the reach of human inquiry, on which the Bible is silent or obscure, Ralegh rejects them as a waste of time and a presumption. He finds the 'scholastical distinctions' of the Schoolmen on such a topic as, say, the text 'The spirit of God moved upon the waters', to be arid and arrogant dissertations, pretensions to a knowledge that could only exist if there were 'no difference between God and man'. Ralegh's refusal to accept the dogma of authority especially on matters he considered above the range of human inquiry, and also the effect of that refusal on conventionally-minded men is beautifully illustrated in his conversation with Ironside, which Ironside reported to the commissioners at Cerne Abbas as an example of 'atheism or apostasy'.

Ironside went to dinner with Sir George Trenchard and found Ralegh and his half-brother Carew Ralegh there among others. Some impudent behaviour of Carew Ralegh's brought reproofs and presumably heated tempers which argued ill for the discussion arising out of the exchange. Ralegh demanded that Ironside should define the nature of the soul, for 'hitherunto in this point (to wit, what the reasonable soul of man is) have I not by any been resolved'. Eventually, Ironside quoted Aristotle that the reasonable soul was 'Actus primus corporis organici animantis humani vitam habentis in potentia'. But this was 'misliked of Sir Walter as obscure and intricate'.

'The reasonable soul', then said Ironside, 'is a spiritual and immortal substance breathed into man by God, whereby he lives and moves and understandeth, and so is distinguished from other creatures.'

> 'Yea, but what is that spiritual and immortal substance breathed into man, etc?' saith Sir Walter.
> 'The soul' quoth I.
> 'Nay, then,' saith he, 'you answer not like a scholar!'

Ironside defended the necessity of this circular reasoning, to be met by Ralegh's claim that definition needed mathematical or demonstrable proof. Ironside rightly objected that such demonstration was impossible with spiritual things, as impossible as with a definition of God. ' "Marry", quoth Sir Walter, "these two be like, for neither could I learn hitherto what God is." ' Ironside accepted Mr. Fitzjames's proffer of Aristotle's definition of 'Ens entium'.

> 'Yea, but what is this *ens entium*?' saith Sir Walter. I answered 'It is God,' and being disliked as before, Sir Walter wished that Grace might be said. 'For that', quoth he, 'is better than this disputation.'

Ralegh's words may seem to show the irreligious jesting of one who had drunk too deep at scientific fountains and who refuses, with stubborn rationalism, to believe in what he cannot measure. Certainly he is seen in a

F

taunting and impatient mood on subjects he need not have been flippant about. But he *has* no patience with those who think they achieve a conclusion by quoting Aristotle or who attempt to define what humanity cannot define. He sets a trap for Ironside and cudgels him when he falls into it. This was the behaviour that won him the title of 'atheist', but we who can turn to the Preface and opening chapters of *The History of the World* can see that what expresses itself so arrogantly in conversation becomes in Ralegh's considered writings a devout humility before the incomprehensibility of God. There are things that cannot be profitably argued about by man nor wholly understood. Philosophers 'spin into small threads, with subtle distinctions, many times, the plainness and sincerity of the scriptures: their wits being like that strong water that eateth thorough and dissolveth the purest gold'.

> Man, to cover his ignorance in the least things, who cannot give a true reason for the grass under his feet, why it should be green rather than red, or of any other colour, that could never yet discover the way and reason of Nature's working in those which are far less noble creatures than himself, who is far more noble than the heavens themselves; Man (saith Solomon) that can hardly discern the things that are upon the earth, and with great labour find out the things that are before us; that hath so short a time in the world as he no sooner begins to learn than to die; that hath in his memory but borrowed knowledge, in his understanding nothing truly; that is ignorant of the essence of his own soul, and which the wisest of the naturalists (if Aristotle be he) could never so much as define but by the action and effect, telling us what it works (which all men know as well as he) but not what it is, which neither he nor any else doth know, save God that created it (*For though* I *were perfect, yet* I *know not my soul*, saith Job)—Man, I say, that is but an idiot in the

next cause of his own life and in the cause of all actions of his life, will notwithstanding examine the art of God in creating the world. . .

Ralegh's Religion

Ralegh's real devotion and belief in God are clear in every section of his *History*. He is not a theologian, but he expresses with power and often with great beauty the traditional medieval view of God and man that found its last great expression in *Paradise Lost*. How his belief that man exists only for union with God in eternity informs his vision of human history will be discussed in Chapter Four. Here we may comment specifically on his expression of the Renaissance tradition of Christian humanism.

Belief in the existence of God, holds Ralegh, is a reasonable thing, even if faith did not teach us. 'As all the rivers in the world, though they have divers risings and divers runnings, though they sometimes hide themselves for a while underground and seem to be lost in sea-like lakes, do at last find and fall into the great ocean; so after all the searches that human capacity hath, and after all philosophical contemplation and curiosity, in the necessity of this Infinite Power, all the reason of man ends and dissolves itself.' But reason is only 'the beginning of knowledge', or it can only confirm what comes from a higher source. Nothing is more mistaken than to perpetuate, as some scholars do, Aubrey's error that Ralegh was a Deist. The nature and purpose of God can only be known in so far as they are revealed through Christ, and though this revelation is everywhere reasonable, 'they grow mad with reason' who endeavour to pursue their inquisition into the essence of God by their own efforts. 'But by his own Word, and by this visible world, is God perceived of men.'

That there is no knowledge of God or of the purpose of life save what is revealed in Scripture, but that the knowledge so gained is not antagonistic to 'natural' thinking, but is indeed everywhere acclaimed and assented to by man's reason, is a typical Christian humanist position—a position which enabled the humanists to fortify the scriptures by the teachings of the pagan writers of ancient Greece and Rome. But we must watch the two uses of the word 'reason'. As I have been using or quoting it, it means 'reasoning power'. But there is also the humanistic 'right reason', which Professor Douglas Bush describes as not an instrument of inquiry, or simply the religious conscience, but 'a kind of rational and philosophic conscience which distinguishes man from the beasts and links man with man and with God'. It is implanted in man to enable him to perceive the law of God. So Ralegh uses the term 'reason' in his discourse on laws (*History of the World*, Book II, Ch. 4) which leans heavily on Augustine and Aquinas. 'To love God, by whom we are, and to do the same right unto all men which we desire should be done unto us, is an effect of the purest reason, in whose highest turrets the quiet of conscience hath made her resting-place and habitation.' Worship of God is human and natural and reasonable; man is made able to receive the knowledge of the law of God. This is the essence of Ralegh's acceptance of Christian humanism. 'As the north-star is the most fixed director of the seaman to his desired port, so is the law of God the guide and conductor of all in general to the haven of eternal life.'

Ralegh accepts without question the fall of man: that God created man for eternal life in union with Himself, that He granted him reason, to be able to know Him and love Him, and free-will to be able to love Him willingly;

that man denied the dictate of his reason, disobeyed God and rejected union. But God of His mercy left the light of right reason burning within man, to be attended to by those with eyes to see and ears to hear, and granted the possibility of salvation even to those who had erred and disobeyed. Almost any chapter of the *History* could be quoted to show how Ralegh believes that the fall of man is continually repeated, that man will sin and deny God in setting before himself objectives in this world which deny the fundamental truth that man is formed only for eternal life. Ralegh is constantly persuading man to reject the magnets of the world and to seek God again. Book I, Chapter Two contains this passage, for example:

> Though nature, according to common understanding, have made us capable by the power of reason, and apt enough, to receive this image of God's goodness which the sensual souls of beasts cannot perceive, yet were that aptitude natural more inclinable to follow and embrace the false and dureless pleasures of this stage-play world than to become the shadow of God, by walking after him; had not the exceeding workmanship of God's wisdom and the liberality of his mercy formed eyes to our souls as to our bodies, which, piercing through the impurity of our flesh, behold the highest heavens, and thence bring Knowledge and Object to the mind and soul, to contemplate the ever-during glory and termless joy prepared for those which retain the image and similitude of their Creator, preserving undefiled and unrent the garment of the new man, which after the image of God is created in righteousness and holiness, as saith St Paul.

It is a strange misreading of Ralegh to suppose that he could believe in God as he did, and believe in the possibility of salvation, without accepting the fact of the Incarnation and the redemption of man through Christ. It is perfectly true that there is little debate in Ralegh's writings on the mystery of the Atonement. He seems to have a temperamental reluctance to explore the doctrine. But to accept a doctrine is not necessarily to dwell upon it. Christ is everywhere 'our Saviour'; there are many specific and devout references to redemption, and even where these are absent, his references to salvation *must* imply Christian doctrine. Most telling of all are his recorded utterances just before his death: Ralegh was not a man for death-bed repentances or one who would avow beliefs he did not hold in order to placate priests. The Dean of Westminster, who attended him in prison, was perfectly satisfied by his speaking 'very Christianly'. Ralegh received the Eucharist on the morning of his execution, and is reported to have said on the scaffold: 'I die in the faith professed by the Church of England. I hope to be saved and have my sins washed away by the precious blood and merits of our saviour Christ.'

Thus the man who stands at the threshold of the modern world in his enthusiasm for the discoveries of modern science and their application can still hold fast to the faith that, though it was central in the formulated beliefs of his age, was rapidly ceasing to be a reality in the lives of men. The conflict between the concept of the world as a divine harmony, the happiness of man depending on his aspiring to play his part in that harmony, and the concept of the world as a material entity to be measured and controlled by man, is the fundamental conflict of the Renaissance. Had Ralegh lived 50 years later he would not have been able to tuck science into a predominantly religious world-view so conveniently as he does; perhaps, like Milton, he would have had to reject scientific inquiry altogether.

Another way of expressing the Renaissance conflict

is to say that it is a conflict between the notion of man as dependent on God and the notion of man as self-sufficient. In these terms we can see how Ralegh manages to find room in himself for both sides of the conflict at almost every turn. Religion and science, humility and pride, desire for wealth and contempt for the world, these can coexist within him as they coexisted in his age. Just as he touches Elizabethan life at every point, so he owns all its contradictions. Active and meditative, tolerant and intolerant, bellicose and pacific, romantic and cynical, humane and cruel, Ralegh *is* the Elizabethan world.

Chapter Three

THE POETRY

(i) GENERAL CHARACTERISTICS

RALEGH'S was not a mind that considered too curiously in poetry, that worried intricate and subtle problems or often took wing on flights of high imagination. He takes broad and general themes and paints with a broad brush. 'Joy' and 'woe' are precise enough emotions for him, and 'sweet spring' and 'parched ground' definite enough images. He chooses the time-honoured commonplaces, the transitoriness of life, the instability of happiness and the impermanence of youth, Time the destroyer, the vanity of desire, love betrayed, corruption in society. It is not for novelty or originality, for brilliance of wit, for the excitement of unconventional concepts, for the recondite, that we turn to Ralegh's poetry; it is for his emphatic, compelling, echoing, re-expression of traditional wisdom.

And what he has to say is all of a piece. In many ways, all Ralegh's poetry is a flowing—a revision and reordering, a working towards the writing of one great poem (so nearly achieved in *Cynthia*). As he rehearses the old sentiments in a new articulation, his memory prompts with phrases and images from former poems. In *Cynthia*, the re-use of poetry written before becomes a deliberate effect. The refrain of 'Farewell to the Court' is 'Of all which past, the sorrow only stays'. In *Cynthia*, he writes:

Twelve years entire I wasted in this war,
  Twelve years of my most happy younger days,
But I in them, and they now wasted are—
  Of all which past, the sorrow only stays.
So wrote I once . . .

It is not in the poetry alone that there is the reappearance of what was said elsewhere. *The History of the World* repeats this same notion of obliterated joy. The seventh age of man is like to Saturn, 'wherein our days are sad and overcast, and in which we find by dear and lamentable experience, and by the loss which can never be repaired, that of all our vain passions and affections past, the sorrow only abideth'. 'A poesie to prove affection is not Love' says:

  Desire himself runs out of breath,
  And getting doth but gain his death.

  .   .   .

  Desire attained is not desire,
  But as the cinders of the fire.

So, in the *Instructions to his Son*, it is affirmed that 'the Desire dieth when it is attained and the Affection perisheth when it is satisfied'.

There are many examples of this trick of repetition, which gives a pleasing harmony to Ralegh's writings— but the most striking is in the well-known 'last poem', written, according to tradition, in his Bible the night before his execution. Ralegh had written, how many years before we do not know, a poem which had begun in his most light-hearted manner about a maiden specially manufactured by Nature for Love, as Spenser's witch produced the false Florimell for her son. The maiden was all of snow and silk and wantonness and wit but, alas, she was given a heart of stone, so Love must die for her whom Nature gave him. But along comes Time, with hands of rusty steel, and pays out the hussy for her hard-heartedness by robbing her of her beauty. In the last stanza, Ralegh, moved to ponder on the way Time destroys *all* beauty, suddenly turns with some indignation against the monster:

> O cruel Time, which takes in trust
>   Our youth, our joys and all we have,
> And pays us but with age and dust,
>   Who, in the dark and silent grave
> When we have wandered all our ways
> Shuts up the story of our days.

Now, as he awaits his death, these lines come into his head and as he transcribes them he transforms them into a moving epitaph which closes with a recognition of that which transcends and overcomes the mutations of Time:

> Even such is Time, which takes in trust
>   Our youth, our joys, and all we have,
> And pays us but with age and dust;
>   Who in the dark and silent grave,
> When we have wandered all our ways,
>   Shuts up the story of our days;
> And from which earth, and grave, and dust,
> The Lord shall raise me up, I trust.

There is great consistency not only in what Ralegh says, but in his style. 'Style', of course, is not something to be detached from a poet's writing to be discussed by itself. Style is expression, is the form of a work, is the means by which a poem says what it does say. The only fruitful discussion of style is really in the analysis of individual works of art, as an explanation of how successfully the poet had made the spirit flesh, by words, images and rhythm and so on. But it is possible and legitimate to talk about some characteristic habits of Ralegh.

Most obvious is the 'solid axiomatical vein', to use Oldys's phrase. Everywhere one finds the emphatic statement, the injunction or admonition in which, with a downright simplicity of diction, Ralegh enforces a traditional truth. The habit had been his from the beginning: the first extant poem that we can date, in commendation of Gascoigne's *Steele Glas*, lives by its 'axiomatic' sentences:

> For whoso reaps renown above the rest
> With heaps of hate shall surely be oppress'd.

The tendency to be insistent, urgent, dogmatic or peremptory spreads throughout the poetry, whether a traditional truth or a piece of homely advice is to be given. The poem 'Conceit begotten by the eyes' is built upon blunt assertions; that fine lyric recently added to the canon, 'Feed still thyself thou fondling with belief', is a series of ironical remonstrances. Sometimes these statements stand singly, designed to have an explosive force; more often, they come together to build up a cumulative, incantatory effect. Like his prose, Ralegh's verse *is* nearly always a building-up; he is rarely a poet from whom single lines can be detached for admiration, the fineness being not in the part but the whole. 'The Lie' is an excellent example of this; it is a surging and compelling progress of imperatives and incisive accusations. 'The Advice' only achieves poetic force by its reiteration through three stanzas of the same notion:

> Many desire, but few or none deserve
>   To win the fort of thy most constant will;
> Therefore take heed, let fancy never swerve
>   But unto him that will defend thee still.
>   For this be sure: the fort of fame once won,
>   Farewell the rest, thy happy days are done.

It is the habit of exclamation that is the cause of one of Ralegh's favourite cadences: a plangent four-syllable phrase, followed by a caesura and a six-syllable resolution.

> Time wears her not, she doth his chariot guide
> Farewell false love, the oracle of lies
> What hath he lost, that so great grace hath won?
> O hopeful love! my object and invention

But although it is easy to pick out a recurrent cadence like this, no complaints can be made against Ralegh for monotony in his rhythms. His skill in achieving special effects by variety of cadences is one of his claims to importance as a poet. Compare, from *Cynthia*,

> No pleasing streams fast to the ocean wending

in which the sound itself flows like the streams, or the languorous line:

> Each living creature draweth to his resting

with the abruptness of:

> But love was gone. So would I, my life were!

or the leaping quality of:

> But that the eyes of my mind held her beams

or the 'onomatopoeic':

> No more than when small drops of rain do fall
> Upon the parched ground by heat updried.

or the adagio of:

> As to the dead, the dead did these unfold.

Simplicity of diction, going with plain obviousness of imagery, is everywhere Ralegh's distinction. Many of the most powerful and dramatic points in *Cynthia* are made with a stark austerity of vocabulary:

All droops, all dies, all trodden under dust

She is gone, she is lost—she is found, she is ever fair!

The thoughts of passed times like flames of hell
Kindled afresh within my memory . . .

Which till all break and all dissolve to dust

Joys under dust that never live again

This unornamented grace of language will be apparent in nearly every quotation to be made. But it is important to remember that so far as *general* simplicity and ease of style go, Ralegh is two poets. In his more private poems, he is turbulent and impulsive and leaps the gates of grammar and logic: in his more public poems there is a carefully ordered lucidity of argument and syntax. A host of examples of the elliptical jumble of the private poem will be found in *Cynthia*.

The simplicity of his words and diction must not tempt us to think of Ralegh as a kind of 'natural' poet, scorning the figures of rhetoric and the poetic devices of his time. In some passages of *Cynthia*, where there is an elaborate patterning of invocation, of apostrophe, of repetition and so on, it is easy for the reader to grasp that Ralegh is obeying conventional rhetorical practices. But it is not so easy to grasp that the *whole* of Ralegh's poetry is obedient to these practices. 'Rhetoric' now has a frightening sense of artificiality about it. The age insisted that a poet should have a thorough grounding in rhetoric: we, with the theories of the Romantic period between us and the Elizabethans, inevitably think that this indicates a false attitude to poetry. We suppose rhetoric to be a garment of poetic diction and false contrivances by which the most prosaic statements could be turned into poetry. In fact, the Renaissance theorists acknowledged as readily as any Romantic poet that there was something divine, something never to be acquired by taking pains, in the inspiration which came to poets. But they argued that it took labour and learning and skill to fashion a poem; as Sidney put it, 'the highest flying wit must have a Daedalus to guide him.' Spontaneous utterance was ill-considered utterance: the arts of poetic discourse were taught to help poets achieve that very different thing, the *air* of spontaneous utterance. Ralegh's *Cynthia*, for example, seems an unstudied outpouring of heart-struck injuries, but it is, instead, a palmary example of the careful control of language and argument which made 'art' seem like 'nature'. In her recent book, *Shakespeare's Use of the Arts of Language*, Sister Miriam Joseph has shown how thoroughly Shakespeare imbibed and employed the techniques of expression advocated in his day by the rhetoricians. His later poetry has not discarded the devices, but has made them so much a part of itself that the triumph of art which perfectly conceals art has been achieved: we praise Shakespeare's later poetry for its 'naturalness and spontaneity'—we should praise it for its art. So it is with Ralegh:

> When she did well, what did there else amiss?
>   When she did ill, what empires could have pleased?
> No other power effecting woe or bliss,
>   She gave, she took, she wounded, she appeased.

This stanza is as thorough-going an employment of conventional rhetorical techniques as the much less seemingly spontaneous lines:

O hopeful love, my object and invention,
   O true desire, the spur of my conceit,
O worthiest spirit, my mind's impulsion,
   O eyes transpersant, my affection's bait,
O princely form, my fancy's adamant,
   Divine conceit, my paines acceptance,
O all in one, O heaven on earth transparent,
   The seat of joys and loves abundance.

Rhetoric was effective expression, and the 'figures' no more than codifications of quite 'natural' modes of speaking.

It is, of course, very hard to say anything to the purpose about Renaissance rhetoric and its relations with poetry in a brief discussion. The subject is large, highly technical and very difficult; it is excellently treated by Miss Rosemond Tuve in her important book, *Elizabethan and Metaphysical Imagery*, and a reader who wants a proper understanding must turn to that book or to Sister Miriam Joseph's work. But one important implication must be understood or much of the value of Ralegh's poetry will be lost. 'Rhetoric' suggests 'stating a case'. Rhetoric is essential to the poet because poetry is communication: poetry is a means of persuading, of arguing of putting a point of view, of explaining an idea. Nearly all Ralegh's lyrics can be seen to be carefully fashioned arguments; they state a case by using whatever devices of rhetoric are applicable to poetry and the particular needs of the poem. The modern reader who comes to poetry expecting 'pure emotion' has much to unlearn and much to learn before he can accept Elizabethan poetry on its own terms. His reward may be that he will discover the Elizabethans to have understood poetry better than any succeeding age. But even if he cannot agree, he must remember that in the best Elizabethan verse, the poetic afflatus provided only the raw material: rhetoric disciplined this raw material into words, images, figures, arguments worthy the high purpose of poetry.

One remarkable feature of Ralegh's verse is the way in which, in his choice of images, he avoids what is remote, subtle or far-fetched. Powerful writer though he is, Ralegh is a plain man's poet: his fancy lingers by the experiences of everyday life, the permanent, the factual. Time and again he draws his metaphors and similes from the sun, dust, fire, blood, the sea, fruit, the shepherd's flock. Some images stand out because they are unusually specific and fanciful, yet in another poet they would seem plain enough. Such an image is in *Cynthia*, when the poet calls memories of the past the 'sorrow-sucking bees' of his sad heart; another is in 'The Lie', where the court 'glows and shines like rotten wood'. It is possible that one has quite enough in Ralegh of fruit falling from the tree and fading flowers, but the great advantage of his simple imagery is that its appeal is immediate: the reader does not dwell on the picture or the idea within the simile or metaphor and so lose the argument of the passage. Images are meant to enforce attention to the meaning of a poem or a passage in a poem and not distract it: Ralegh's images, never startling and rarely unexpected, succeed in this.

It is in keeping with the broad and plain imagery that the verse should contain many simple personifications. Almost from a medieval allegory is such a picture as this:

> And at my gate Despair shall linger still
> To let in Death, when Love and Fortune will.

'Desire' runs out of breath, 'Oblivion' lays him down on Laura's hearse, 'Mercy' is fled to God which Mercy made.

Briefly to sum up a brief account, Ralegh's verse always returns to the same few themes, most of which can be included within the single title, 'Mutability'. He dispenses traditional morality, painting bold colours with a firm hand, his manner imperative and insistent. Although his language and imagery are very simple and direct, generally free from 'Petrarchan' excesses, his work is nevertheless obedient to the rhetorical requirements of his day. Paradoxically, this 'plain man's poet' can, in poems of a more private kind, be almost intolerably difficult.

(ii) THE LYRICS

Ralegh's major lyrics are all didactic, imparting a sage's experience of life. They vary greatly in their mood, from sombre to flippant, avuncular to homiletic, but in one way or another all are concerned with Love and Time.

An attack on a false conception of love is found in 'Conceit begotten by the eyes', a fine lyric that is in a way another answer to Marlowe, if we think of the latter's lines:

> The reason no man knows, let it suffice
> What we behold is censured by our eyes:
> Where both deliberate, the love is slight—
> Who ever loved that loved not at first sight?

Ralegh's poem sternly begins:

> Conceit begotten by the eyes
> Is quickly born and quickly dies;
> For while it seeks our hearts to have,
> Meanwhile there reason makes his grave.

G

'Conceit' is a fancy which has to do only with the
emotions and outward appearances, and it leads only to
'affection', that is to say, infatuation or mere passion.
Love of this sort, which has nothing to do with the mind
and the judgment, has no real root and no stability. It
betrays its meretriciousness in that, unlike true love, the
possession of its object brings not joy but disgust and its
own death.

> Affection follows Fortune's wheels,
> And soon is shaken from her heels;
> For, following beauty or estate,
> Her liking still is turned to hate.
> For all affections have their change,
> And Fancy only loves to range.
>
> Desire himself runs out of breath,
> And getting, doth but gain his death;
> Desire nor reason hath nor rest,
> And blind doth seldom choose the best;
> Desire attained is not desire,
> But as the cinders of the fire.

The poem ends with scorn for those poets who pretend
that this irrational infatuation is 'perfect love':

> As if wild beasts and men did seek
> To like, to love, to choose alike.

False love is also shown up in 'The Advice'. Beneath
the heavy and prudent injunctions lies a distinction
between lust, the ephemeral desire that seeketh only
self to please, and more permanent emotion.

A similar distinction, between a fickle and unconstant
emotion and real love, is sharply drawn in 'Walsingham'.
This is the most haunting and magical of Ralegh's poems.
It is based upon an old ballad, snatches of which Ophelia
sings in her madness. In rewriting it, Ralegh has lost

none of its savour. Besides its own intrinsic value, the lyric is important as a kind of summing-up of *Cynthia*; it expresses with terse power the anguish of rejection, the complaint against the changeableness of one kind of love and the belief in the unchangeableness of another, which *Cynthia* describes at length. The whole poem is worth quoting.

'As you came from the holy land
    Of Walsinghame,
Met you not with my true love
    By the way as you came?'

'How shall I know your true love,
    That have met many one
As I went to the holy land,
    That have come, that have gone?'

'She is neither white nor brown
    But as the heavens fair,
There is none hath a form so divine
    In the earth or the air.'

'Such an one did I meet, good Sir,
    Such an angel-like face,
Who like a queen, like a nymph, did appear,
    By her gait, by her grace.'

'She hath left me here all alone,
    All alone as unknown,
Who sometimes did me lead with herself
    And me loved as her own.'

'What's the cause that she leaves you alone
    And a new way doth take,
Who loved you once as her own
    And her joy did you make?'

'I have loved her all my youth,
　　But now old, as you see,
Love likes not the falling fruit
　　From the withered tree.'

'Know that love is a careless child
　　And forgets promise past;
He is blind, he is deaf when he list,
　　And in faith never fast.

His desire is a dureless content
　　And a trustless joy;
He is won with a world of despair
　　And is lost with a toy.'

'Of women-kind such indeed is the love,
　　Or the word 'love' abused,
Under which many childish desires
　　And conceits are excused.

But true love is a durable fire
　　In the mind ever burning:
Never sick, never old, never dead,
　　From itself never turning.'

In this poem the themes of Love and Mutability are
united. The last stanza hints at something which has the
power to outgo and withstand Time. True love, firmly
rooted in the mind as well as the emotions, enduring in
spite of all vicissitudes and tribulations, is explained in
Cynthia to be a man's 'cause of being'. By this unquenchable love for the 'angel-like' beings of the earth (with
all their infidelity), the soul takes 'immortal kind'.

Others of the major lyrics have a predominant strain
of *de contemptu mundi*, stressing that it is not the material
world, changeable, troublesome, untrustworthy, spe-

cious, that demands the mind's attention and heart's devotion. 'What is our life? a play of passion' is an extended comparison of life to the theatre and stresses the unimportance and evanescence of all that we are involved in in this 'short comedy' of our lives:

> Thus march we playing to our latest rest—
> Only we die in earnest, that's no jest.

Every material enticement and physical joy that youth offers to youth in Marlowe's 'Come live with me and be my love', Ralegh in his rejoinder points out to be under the tyranny of Time; to imagine that happiness abides in them is to be 'in folly ripe, in reason rotten'.

It is worth noting that although Ralegh, when he is in this mood, wishes to inculcate a disregard for earthly glories and turn men's eyes to realities beyond the material world, he can also portray with perfect sympathy the pathos of man's helplessness against the wrackful siege of battering days. He can be angry with Time as well as despise its power. The speed with which he can turn from chiding those who can look no higher than the passing shows of the world to a mood of pity and regret that all on earth is a prey to ineluctable time is well seen in the stanza I have quoted earlier from 'Nature that wash'd her hands in milk'. The elegiac note which suddenly appears at the end of the poem is all the more poignant because it is so unexpected.

The best poem *de contemptu mundi* is probably 'The Lie'. This is like a series of relentless swordthrusts. It proclaims how all on earth is corrupt and tainted. Here are a few stanzas:

> Go soul the body's guest
>   Upon a thankless errand:
> Fear not to touch the best,
>   The truth shall be thy warrant.

Go, since I needs must die,
And give the world the lie.

Say to the Court it glows
    And shines like rotten wood;
Say to the Church it shows
    What's good, and doth no good.
        If Church and Court reply,
        Then give them both the lie.

. . . . . .

Tell men of high condition,
    That manage the estate,
Their purpose is ambition,
    Their practice only hate;
        And if they once reply,
        Then give them all the lie.

. . . . . .

Tell zeal it wants devotion,
    Tell love it is but lust;
Tell time it meets but motion,
    Tell flesh it is but dust;
        And wish them not reply,
        For thou must give the lie.

Tell age it daily wasteth,
    Tell honour how it alters;
Tell beauty how she blasteth,
    Tell favour how it falters;
        And as they shall reply,
        Give every one the lie.

. . . . . .

So when thou hast, as I
    Commanded thee, done blabbing,
Although to give the lie
    Deserves no less than stabbing,
        Stab at thee he that will,
        No stab thy soul can kill.

The ending note of the poem is the same as that of the epitaph, 'Even such is Time'; in both places Ralegh hints at the faith which puts the perturbations of earthly change into their proper perspective:

> And from which earth, and grave, and dust,
> The Lord shall raise me up, I trust.

Shakespeare's treatment of Love and Time in his Sonnets has as its summation the similar assurance:

> So shalt thou feed on death that feeds on men,
> And death once dead, there's no more dying then.

I have suggested, in mentioning the importance of rhetoric, that a pouring forth of the emotions was not what Ralegh's age thought poetry. It is very hard to find a single lyric of Ralegh's which is a simple record of personal feeling, although many are written in the first person and often speak of the poet's grief. In explaining why the 'I' of such poems—and (later) of *Cynthia*—is not to be taken as Ralegh, nor the emotions expressed literally his, it may seem I am doing him disservice and detracting from his sincerity as a poet. Sincerity in Elizabethan poetry is very generally misunderstood. There is, for example, the question of plagiarism. Ralegh's sonnet 'Like to a hermit poor in place obscure' is, like so many sonnets of the period, borrowed from a continental source—here, from Desportes. If the borrowing is so extensive as to be virtually a translation (as here), it is a common reaction to dismiss the work as a 'literary exercise'; if the borrowing is more of an idea, or a conceit only, the poet is accused of false sentiment and insincerity. But Elizabethan poets had not been nurtured on the belief that to be true to oneself was to be quite different and independent from anyone else. The Elizabethan dramatist was an unrepentant 'plagiarist' if he found in an old story a fitting vehicle for something he wished to express. So the sonneteer went to the continental masters to find suitable expressions of his own thoughts and moods; more often, since no-one had then conceived the notion that a lyric should be a confession on oath, he went to the continental sonnet to find thoughts which he considered worthy to be enshrined in his own language.

In this particular sonnet I think it was Ralegh's own personal feeling which led him to the French poem; as he translates it, he makes departures from the original which make it more akin to what we may imagine to have been Ralegh's own mood. The resulting poem is neither a literary exercise nor insincere: it is a rendering into verse of certain notions, found in a French model, for which Ralegh felt some personal sympathy.

The 'sincerity' of the love-lyrics presents other problems. Two of them ('The Excuse' and 'Our passions are most like to floods and streams') stand out among Ralegh's rather morose poetry for their good-humour and gaiety, but the field is neither big enough nor good enough for a long discussion. What has to be remembered is that these poems, like so many Elizabethan love-lyrics, subordinate 'truth' to two things: complimenting the mistress and 'proving' by ingenious logic that the poet loves the mistress. This compliment or this proof is the purpose of the poems; they must not be frowned upon because they fail to live up to requirements not of their age.

What normally happens in Ralegh's personal poems (including *Cynthia*) is that the 'I' in the poem becomes generalised. The poet 'transmutes his personal and private agonies into something rich and strange, something

universal and impersonal', to use Mr. Eliot's phrase.
'Even such is Time' is not merely a cry from the heart,
but a reflection on 'the human condition'. It seems to me
that to show how a poet enlarges a statement about himself into something more general is not to show him being
insincere. I shall take one lyric to show the relation
between the speaker and the poet, and also to show something of the rhetorical organisation of a lyric. It is in
Ralegh's own handwriting in the Hatfield House manuscript:

> My body in the walls captived
>> Feels not the wounds of spiteful envy,
> But my thralled mind, of liberty deprived,
>> Fast fettered in her ancient memory,
> Doth naught behold but sorrow's dying face;
>> Such prison erst was so delightful
> As it desired no other dwelling place,
>> But time's effects, and destinies despiteful,
> Have changed both my keeper and my fare;
>> Love's fire and beauty's light I then had store,
> But now close kept, as captives wonted are,
>> That food, that heat, that light, I find no more.
>>> Despair bolts up my doors, and I alone
>>> Speak to dead walls, but those hear not my moan.

The poem is a prisoner's complaint, and Ralegh was
indeed a prisoner when he wrote it: it is almost certain
that the poems in this manuscript belong to the period in
1592 when Elizabeth's displeasure with Ralegh for his
marriage sent him to the Tower (see p. 99). But the
prisoner is speaking of lost *love*, not the lost regard and
favour of the Queen. Ralegh has generalized his particular emotion: not the dismissed Captain of the Guard,
but the universal lorn lover speaks. Personal grief
inspires the poem, but again, the *purpose* of the poem is not

to describe personal grief, but to explore the difference between real and apparent constraint, on the basis of an extended image of the prison.

First he states that stone walls do not a prison make: his body does not suffer from his present restraint—it is his mind that is suffering, fettered as it is to the memory of one who formerly loved him. But it is not because his mind is in bondage that he is now so wretched, since it has long been the servant of her he loves, and he had formerly found in that mental servitude a perfect freedom. No: the rigours of his present imprisonment lie in a mental servitude without the warmth of affection returned. He is like a prisoner who does not object to his cell, as such, but finds the cold and darkness intolerable. Not bodily restraint, not the restraint of the soul in being devoted, but the helplessness of loving one who repudiates him is the true deprivation and entombment. It is this despair that 'bolts up my doors'; his beloved's hard-heartedness and refusal to yield to entreaty are the walls which shut him in.

It is therefore not enough to label this poem a poem of private emotion. It is that and more than that: it becomes generalized when the dismissed courtier becomes the rejected lover, and it is made objective when an emotional state becomes the subject of intellectual analysis.

The most highly polished of Ralegh's lyrics are the occasional poems, commendatory or obsequial. They were the only poems destined for the public and for posterity. The best are the epitaph on Sir Philip Sidney and the first of the two poems in commendation of *The Faerie Queene*. The epitaph on Sidney has simplicity, grace, dignity and restraint and conveys a sense of the public's loss; hardly one of the great English elegies, it yet succeeds where so many have embarrassingly failed by its unpretentiousness and its refusal to invent a personal grief where one was not apparently deeply felt. A poem that *is*, however, among the greatest of its kind in English is the 'Vision upon this conceit of the Faerie Queene':

> Methought I saw the grave where Laura lay,
>   Within that temple where the vestal flame
> Was wont to burn, and passing by that way
>   To see that buried dust of living fame,
> Whose tomb fair Love and fairer Virtue kept,
>   All suddenly I saw the Faery Queen,
> At whose approach the soul of Petrarch wept,
>   And from thenceforth those Graces were not seen,
> For they this Queen attended, in whose stead
>   Oblivion laid him down on Laura's hearse;
> Hereat the hardest stones were seen to bleed
>   And groans of buried ghosts the heavens did pierce
>   Where Homer's sprite did tremble all for grief
>   And curst th' access of that celestial thief.

Pictorial vividness is not necessarily a criterion of good poetry but this sonnet is a 'vision', and it is a tribute to Ralegh's success that he has, like an Elizabethan miniaturist, presented in a mere fourteen lines, each detail sharp in small compass, the dream-world the medieval allegorists loved to invent. The sonnet moves in stately fashion as befits its 'regal' subject, and the variation in the pauses, the playing off of the rhythmic unit of the line against the rhythmic unit of the phrase are both contrived more subtly than we normally find they are: the alliteration, too, is much less obtrusive and more effective than usual. The vocabulary and imagery have that power of simplicity and directness that is Ralegh's great strength. One cannot be very sure about the extent to

which the vowel sounds have been consciously arranged
but certainly pleasing effects are achieved; there is, for
example, the linking of an end-rhyme, 'seen', with the
medial 'Queen' in the next line, and it is hard to believe
that it was by accident that the chiming of the vowels
came about in these two lines:

> Hereat the hardest stones were seen to bleed
> And groans of buried ghosts the heavens did pierce.[1]

The 'Petition to Queen Anne' is an occasional poem,
though not a 'public' poem. It is a late and mature work
and we are lucky to possess what is almost certainly
an earlier draft, 'My day's delight, my springtime joys
foredone', which helps us to see how Ralegh tightens
up his work in revision. Although the final version is
undoubtedly an improvement, much of worth has been
excised. A brief statement takes the place of a 24-line
development of one of Ralegh's favourite themes—the
inconstancy of friendship, that alters when it alteration
finds:

> Moss to unburied bones, ivy to walls
>   Whom life and people have abandoned,
> Till th' one be rotten, stays, till th' other falls,
>
> But friendships, kindred and love's memory
>   Dies sole, extinguished, hearing or beholding
> The voice of woe or face of misery.

The 'Petition' itself has more dignity than some of
Ralegh's appeals for restoration of liberty; he concen-
trates more on the person he is addressing than on himself, and avoids the more querulously personal note as

[1] In talking about the value of vowel sounds one has to take into account
not only the differences of Elizabethan pronunciation from our own, but also
the special differences of Ralegh's 'broad Devonshire'.

he talks of the submersion of truth, the decay of mercy, the fickleness of friendship and so on. There are some fine lines: one has that simplicity and obviousness, almost toppling over into banality, which is so often found in Ralegh and can be so effective in its context:

> For what we sometimes were, we are no more

The last of the lyrics to be considered is perhaps the best-known of all, 'The passionate man's pilgrimage, supposed to be written by one at the point of death'. Actually, it is only the first few and last few lines that are well-known and often quoted:

> Give me my scallop-shell of quiet,
> My staff of faith to walk upon,
> My scrip of joy, immortal diet,
> My bottle of salvation,
> My gown of glory, hope's true gage,
> And thus I'll take my pilgrimage.

> . . . . . .

> And this is my eternal plea
> To Him that made heaven, earth and sea:
> Seeing my flesh must die so soon
> And want a head to dine next noon,
> Just at the stroke when my veins start and spread,
> Set on my soul an everlasting head;
> Then am I ready like a palmer fit
> To tread those blest paths which before I writ.

If the lines that fall between these two passages were more often read, Ralegh's authorship might sometimes be questioned. But even in the lines quoted, is there not a feeling of strangeness? The lovely image of the scallop-shell is unusually fanciful and decorative for Ralegh, and perhaps less functional than is usual with him. And in the last lines, though Ralegh could have joked as well as anyone about his expected decapitation, the wit of 'and want a head to dine next noon' is foreign to him. It is too grotesque and bizarre, and belongs to a school of poetry which was not Ralegh's. The same may be said of the punning in the lines about Christ as attorney:

> Who pleads for all without degrees
> And He hath angels—but no fees.

Throughout the poem, both the religious sense and the imagery seem most unlike Ralegh. It is not that the poem is wholly concerned with salvation through Christ's redemption—I have argued that Ralegh's religion is orthodox enough—but that the sense of personal relationship with Christ and the emotional response to the Atonement, which are at the very heart of the poem, are things not found anywhere else in Ralegh's work. Could he have written:

> Blood must be my body's balmer

where 'blood' is the pilgrim's blood and perhaps Christ's blood, given once as a ransom for mankind, and given again in the Eucharist? Ralegh generally seems averse to dwelling upon mysteries—even if he believes in them. As for the personal note, take the lines:

> Christ pleads his death, and then we live:
> Be thou my speaker, taintless pleader,
> Unblotted lawyer, true proceeder;
> Thou movest salvation even for alms.

The imagery is everywhere at one with the religious tone: to some it will suggest a member of the Roman rather than of the Protestant church:

> I'll bring them first
> To slake their thirst,
> And then to taste those nectar suckets
> > At the clear wells
> > Where sweetness dwells
> Drawn up by saints in crystal buckets.

'Nectar fountains', 'milken hill', 'the holy paths'—

> > Strewed with rubies thick as gravel,
> > Ceilings of diamonds, sapphire floors,
> > High walls of coral and pearly bowers,

—could Ralegh's pictorial fancy or his devotion flow in these images? It is not only the presence of a foreign type of imagery but the absence of the expected type that puzzles me in this poem. Lines which do not speak against Ralegh do not speak unhesitatingly for him. Such lines are:

> My staff of faith to walk upon

> My soul will be a-dry before,
> But after, it will ne'er thirst more.

Although the diction is often simple enough to be Ralegh's, the rhythms are unusual—particularly the rocking rhythm of the following couplet:

> Then the holy paths we'll travel,
> Strew'd with rubies thick as gravel

Another foreign note is struck in the rather naive sociability of the poem at one point:

> And by the happy blissful way,
> > More peaceful pilgrims I shall see
> That have shook off their gowns of clay
> > And go apparel'd fresh like me.
> I'll bring them first
> To slake their thirst . . .

Ralegh generally addresses his poetry with some sternness to his audience—or to himself. This friendly spirit, this *we*, rather than *I* or *you*, seems a little outside Ralegh the man and the poet.

The poem is one that, in spite of unevenness and occasional silliness, has great beauty and richness of feeling and sparks of magnificence. It first appeared as an appendage to *Daiphantus*, by 'An.Sc.' in 1604, but, as Miss Latham remarks, a 'strong manuscript tradition' assigns it to Ralegh; there is no evidence of any other author. Every artist may produce a work quite unlike all his others, and Ralegh may have stepped outside himself to write this, but I like to think that evidence may come to light to support my strong impression that the author is not Ralegh, but another who lay under the shadow of the scaffold.

(iii) THE OCEAN TO CYNTHIA[1]

The Composition of the Poem

At Hatfield House there was found in the 1860's a manuscript in Ralegh's handwriting containing a poem of 522 lines headed 'The 21th: and last booke of the Ocean to Scinthia', a fragment entitled 'The end of the bookes, of the Oceans love to Scinthia, and the beginninge of the 22 Boock, entreatinge of Sorrow'.[2] There is also the enigmatic 'If Cynthia be a Queen, a princess, and

---

[1] The problems concerning Ralegh's 'Cynthia' poetry are admirably and succinctly reviewed by Miss Latham in the introduction to her 1951 edition of the poems, and the reader who wishes for a fuller survey of the facts behind Ralegh's most considerable poetic work than is contained in the following review should turn to her account.

[2] I for a long time accepted Miss Latham's contention (1951 ed., p. 122) that the numerals must be '11th' and '12th', because the 'th' is clear and because Ralegh would be likely to work to a scheme of twelve books to a long poem. But further examination has brought me back to the old reading: it is hard to think the first digit is anything but 2. Mr. I. A. Shapiro informs me (supporting J. P. Gibson, *Review of English Studies*, 1928, p. 340) that '21th' would be a common way of writing 'one and twentieth'.

The 21: and last booke of
the Ocean to Scinthia

Suffireth it to yow my ioyes interred.
in simpell wordes that I my woes cumplayne,
yow that then died when first my fancy erred.
ioyes vnder dust that neuer liue agayne.
If to the liuinge weare my muse adressed.
or did my minde her own spirit still inhold.
weare not my liuinge passion so repressed,
as to the dead, the dead did thes vnfold,
sume sweeter wordes, sume more beseming verse
should wittness my mishapp in hygher kynd.
but my loues wounds, my fancy in the hearse,
the Idea but restinge, of a wasted minde.
the blossumes fallen, the sapp gon from the tree.
the broken monuments of my great desires.
from thes so lost what may th affections bee,
to that heat in Cynders of extinguisht fiers.
Lost in the mudd of thos hygh flowinge streames
which through more fayrer feilds ther courses bend,
slayne with self thoughts, amasde in fearfull dreames,
woes without date, discumforts without ond,
from frutfull trees I gather withred leaues
and glean the broken eares with misers hands
who sumetyme did injoy the waighty sheues

Basan, or Basanitis regio, over Jordan, in longth from the
torrent Jabor to the confines of Getrha, of the Gessuri &
Marchati in breadth, from the hills Galaad, Seir, & Hermon,
to ye sea of Galile & Jordan.   Basan signifieth fatt &
fruitfull, exceeding in goodly oakes, & therfore was it sayd
querous basan. It was also called terra Rephaim. id est
gigantū. Ane yeere after Chodorlahomor had slayne
the kings of Sodom & Basan. Og, being of y race of Rephaim
obtayned that region called Basanitidis, in wth ther
were 60 Citties wald. all wth fair the soome of Menasse
retonered & siow Og & his soonns. & called them siuoth fair,
or the Citties of fair. & were Geuen by Moses to the half
tribe of Manasse.

Deut. 3.

Numb. 32.
deut. 3.
Josua. 13. c
17.

1. Edrai, the seat of Og.
2. Corozaim.
3. Cedar.
4. Ashroth.
5. Gamala
6. Galaad.
7. Pella
8. faber galaad.
9. Hippos
10. Ephron.
11. Gatton.
12. Gerasa.

A page of Ralegh's notes for The History of the World

supreme' and the sonnet 'My body in the walls captived.'
That Ralegh had written a poem of some consequence
to Elizabeth as 'Cynthia' had been well-known before this
discovery. The evidence, apart from a reference of
Gabriel Harvey's to 'Sir Walter Ralegh's Cynthia', came
from Edmund Spenser. When Ralegh went to look after
his estates in Ireland in 1589, it was commonly rumoured
that he had left the Court in disgrace; the hectic tone
of his denials of this rumour add to rather than diminish
our feeling that the Queen was indeed 'in the frown'.
While he was in Ireland, Ralegh became a friend of
Spenser, who has left in his poem of courtly compliment,
Colin Clouts Come Home Again, a record of an intimacy that
eventually led to Ralegh's introducing Spenser and his
Faerie Queene to Elizabeth.

A 'straunge shepheard', says Spenser, chanced to find
him out:

> Himselfe he did ycleepe
> The shepheard of the Ocean by name,
> And said he came far from the main-sea deepe;
> He, sitting me beside in that same shade,
> Provoked me to plaie some pleasant fit;
> And, when he heard the musicke which I made,
> He found himselfe full greatly pleasd at it:
> Yet, æmuling my pipe, he tooke in hond
> My pipe, before that æmuled of many,
> And plaid thereon (for well that skill he cond),
> Himselfe as skilfull in that art as any.
> He pip'd, I sung; and, when he sung, I piped,
> By chaunge of turnes, each making other mery . . .
> . . . .
> His song was all a lamentable lay
> Of great unkindnesse, and of usage hard,
> Of *Cynthia* the Ladie of the Sea,
> Which from her presence faultlesse him debard.

H

And ever and anon, with singults rife,
He cryed out, to make his undersong:
'Ah my loves queene, and goddesse of my life,
Who shall me pittie, when thou doest me wrong?'

. . . . . .

Right well he sure did plaine
That could great *Cynthiaes* sore displeasure breake,
And move to take him to her grace againe.

Ralegh's 'Cynthia' is mentioned elsewhere by Spenser:
in the prefatory stanzas to Book Three of the *Faerie
Queene*, Spenser thus addresses his 'Dredd Soveraigne':

But if in living colours and right hew
Thyselfe thou covet to see pictured,
Who can it doe more lively, or more trew,
Then that sweete verse, with Nectar sprinckeled,
In which a gracious servaunt pictured
His *Cynthia*, his heavens fayrest light?
That with his melting sweetnes ravished,
And with the wonder of her beames bright,
My sences lulled are in slomber of delight.

Again, in one of the sonnets 'to Various Noblemen, &c'
prefixed to his epic, Spenser says to Ralegh:

Yet till that thou thy Poeme wilt make knowne,
Let thy faire Cinthias praises bee thus rudely showne.

The dedication to *Colin Clout* is dated 1591, and
although the poem was not published until 1595, there is
no reason to suppose that the references to Ralegh were
changed after the original composition and before publication. The first three books of *The Faerie Queene* were
published in 1590. All Spenser's remarks presumably
refer, therefore, to poetry or a poem that Ralegh had
written or was writing when he was with Spenser in
1589. This poetry is addressed to the Queen and extols
her but also complains of her harshness. It had been

influential in restoring Ralegh to the Queen's favour, apparently by 1591.

It seems most improbable that this poem is the poem we possess: our *Cynthia* has no 'undersong', and there is hardly sufficient praise of Elizabeth in it to make it safe for the aspiring Spenser to recommend it to his sovereign as a true and lively picture of her. Our *Cynthia* begins with the 'twenty-first book', and although that does not necessarily mean that the earlier books had all been written, at least it suggests that earlier material has been lost. Again, of all periods that are likely to have inspired the intense emotion which permeates the extant book, none is more suitable than a period well after Spenser's references, the period of imprisonment, in utter disgrace, following Ralegh's marriage in 1592. This later date is made even more probable if we suppose that all the Hatfield House poems belong to the same period; 'My body in the walls captived' can refer only to a period of imprisonment.

Miss Latham has suggested that *Cynthia* was a 'cumulative poem, written over a period of years, and that the "lamentable lay" which Spenser heard, and which was provoked by the events of 1589, was no more than the latest instalment.' This is a very attractive notion, and it is possible, if the earlier *Cynthia* consists of a series of laments and rhapsodies, that we can lay our hands on some of them. Earlier writing to the Queen is quoted or invoked in the surviving Book (ll. 45-6, 123-131, 344-355)[1] and there are four extant lyrics which may well have formed part of a sequence to the Queen.

[1] In six passages in the Hatfield Book, each line in the manuscript commences with a marginal mark, thus =. Miss Latham (1951, p. 126) suggests that these marks are like the inverted commas which call attention to rhetorical passages. But since all three passages which openly hark back to earlier writing are thus marked, it seems to me probable that they always denote quotations by Ralegh from his former poetry, perhaps the early *Cynthia*.

Three of these poems are sonnets: 'Prais'd be Diana's fair and harmless light', 'Like truthless dreams, so are my joys expired' and 'Those eyes which set my fancy on a fire'. It is very likely indeed that Ralegh joined in the vogue for sonnet-sequences in order to express his devotion to the Queen. The second two quatrains of the first sonnet (it is irregular in form) are of the very stuff of the later *Cynthia*—the adoring part of it, at least:

> In heaven Queen she is among the spheres,
>> In aye she mistress-like makes all things pure;
> Eternity in her oft change she bears,
>> She beauty is: by her the fair endure.
> Time wears her not, she doth his chariot guide;
>> Mortality below her orb is placed,
> By her the virtue of the stars down glide,
>> In her is virtue's perfect image cast.

'Those eyes which set my fancy on a fire' is a perfectly conventional sonnet of praise and is just the sort of poem that Ralegh might be referring to in the Hatfield Book when he says:

> Out of that mass of miracles, my Muse
>> Gathered those flowers, to her pure senses pleasing;
> Out of her eyes, the store of joys, did choose
>> Equal delights, my sorrows counterpoising.

The third of these lyrics, the very moving 'farewell to the Court' ('Like truthless dreams') has its undersong, 'Of all which past, the sorrow only stays', and this is quoted again in the Hatfield Book with application to new disillusionment. Its theme is a central 'Cynthia' theme: the bitter insistence that happiness and joy are blotted out as though they had never been by the woe that inevitably follows them; the heart cannot store them and pay dividends in the later time of sadness; joy is only a 'truthless dream'. Edmund Gosse (*The Athenaeum*,

January 1886) suggested that this poem had in another version formed part of the early *Cynthia*.

'Feed still thyself thou fondling with belief', from the 1593 anthology *The Phoenix Nest*, is a recent candidate for admission to the Ralegh canon, and is perhaps the most convincingly Raleghan poem of the group disinterred from *The Phoenix Nest* by recent scholarship. In intensity it is at a level with 'The Lie'. It is a savage 'struggling from love's subjection' and recalls one striking mood of the later *Cynthia*, the metre of which it shares. The poet bitterly accuses himself for having pursued a love that could only come to grief, for still clinging by the old attraction even when it has brought him to unhappiness, for persuading himself, in 'dreams of wish and vain desire', that all is not lost, for making little of the humiliation he has endured at his mistress' hands, and for complaining of fortune when his own wilfulness and blindness are to blame. Whether or no this lyric does form part of the early 'lamentable lay' it is surely inspired by Ralegh's hatred of himself for being so at the mercy of his devotion to the Queen even when she has slighted him.

It is suggested, then, that the extant poem to Cynthia belongs to 1592, when Ralegh was in the Tower, and that the poetry to the Queen mentioned by Spenser belongs to an earlier date, and that though much of it has been lost, fragments of it may exist among Ralegh's lyrics and sonnets.[1]

[1] Since this chapter was written, there has been an interesting addition to the story of *Cynthia*. At the back of his notebook (see pp. 48 and 147), Ralegh has inscribed a most lovely lyric which is a kind of envoy to the *Cynthia* cycle:

> Now we have present made
> To Cynthia . . .

See facsimile, with transcript and notes by G. Seddon, *Illustrated London News*, February 28, 1953.

Obstacles and Conventions

In *The Ocean to Cynthia*, one who is wretched in having lost the affection of a mistress he has long served with intense devotion, dwells painfully on his sorrow, laments the happiness that has gone and meditates on the vicissitudes of love and fortune. The poem is a fevered elegy, obscure, turbulent and erratic, with the incoherence almost of delirium in the flow of its thought. There is nothing like it elsewhere in Elizabethan poetry.

Some of the difficulties and obscurities are due, in all probability, to the fact that the poem is not in its final state. In our manuscript, Ralegh is transcribing an earlier draft (Latham, 1951 edition, p. 124) and he is clearly making changes as he copies, but that the transcript cannot represent the poem in a finished state is obvious both from the appearance of the manuscript and from internal evidence. There are a good many ink-marks which must be tokens of dissatisfaction, or reminders to revise. The uneasy word 'groans' in l. 285 is marked for alteration, and so is the ambiguous 'my love was false', in l. 465.

Any printed version which divides the poem up into the quatrains of which it is composed will show at a glance how many times a quatrain is left uncompleted, sometimes leaving a sentence uncompleted also; four times, a metrically otiose line has crept in. These are loose ends that could have been quickly tidied up. Sometimes the irregularity has occurred because lines have been erased, and nothing substituted to complete the rhyme-scheme (*e.g.* l. 331). Ralegh has realised that the metre has gone wrong at 150–4, and has made two strokes in the margin to mark the error. There is one rather interesting example of significant irregularity in

the stanza form. From l. 376 the poem mounts in a
sustained march to the great climax of 408–415, on the
theme of:

> A love obscured but cannot be forgotten,
> Too great and strong for Time's jaws to devour.

At line 400 he states that nothing that happened to Cynthia
could alter his devotion:

> Which never change to sad adversity,
> > Which never age, or nature's overthrow,
> Which never sickness or deformity,
> > Which never wasting care or wearing woe
> If subject unto these she could have been . . . .

> Which never words or wits malicious,
> > Which never honour's bait or world's fame
> Achieved by attempts adventurous,
> > Or aught beneath the sun or heaven's frame,
> Can so dissolve, dissever or destroy—

The four dots and the rule drawn across the page are
from Ralegh's manuscript. Repetition of initial words in
successive lines is one of Ralegh's favourite figures: it is
the interruption of the figure by the fifth line of the
quotation that strikes the reader almost before he notices
the interruption of the quatrain rhyme-scheme. What is
more likely than that Ralegh, transcribing his lines, saw
that he had been carried away and had contradicted an
earlier remark (183–192) that his love was superior to
the ravages of Time, and, on a more material level, had
made certain of offending the Queen he sought to
appease by suggesting that she was liable to the decay of
old age? Poetically and politically, he had stumbled, and
a line is hastily inserted with a mark to remind him to
return to the passage later to find a way of 'perishing

the thought' without interrupting the flow of the verse.
A larger interpolation is the passage 193–200. Ralegh
has been exalting Cynthia in the highest terms:

> A spring of beauties which time ripeth not—
> Time that but works on frail mortality,
>
> .   .   .   .   .   .
>
> Blossoms of pride that can not fade nor fall

Then, suddenly, a note of bitter sarcasm not found elsewhere appears:

> These were those marvellous perfections,
>   The parents of my sorrow and my envy;
> Most deathful and most violent infections:
>   These be the tyrants that in fetters tie
> Their wounded vassals, yet nor kill nor cure
>   But glory in their lasting misery
> That as her beauties would our woes should dure,
>   These be the effects of powerful empery . . . .

Again the dots are Ralegh's. It seems possible that Ralegh
stopped at this point and asked himself if he had not
given rein to too much bitterness. He leaves a space in
the manuscript and starts again with one of his rare capital
letters, leaving unerased the passage just quoted: the next
line in the poem follows in sense not 'These be the
effects of powerful empery' but the earlier 'Blossoms of
pride that can nor fade nor fail':

> Yet have these wonders want which want compassion,
>   Yet hath her mind some marks of human race,
> Yet will she be a woman for a fashion,
>   So doth she please her virtues to deface.

And he continues in this strain for nine lines more. This
is better: he has excised the rancour and substituted a
very satisfying paradox of Cynthia's having both the

virtues of a goddess and the fickleness of a woman. But
perhaps Ralegh is uncertain of the rightness of this second
version also, is undecided whether at this point he
should criticise Cynthia at all, for the poem takes up
again (213), with a capital letter in the manuscript once
more:

> But leave her praise, speak thou of naught but woe,
> Write on the tale that Sorrow bids thee tell
>
> . . . . . .
>
> Describe her now as she appears to thee,
> Not as she did appear in days foredone.

By no stretching of terms can either of the two passages
which follow 'Blossoms of pride . . .' be called *praise*.
Both passages may have been intended for excision, and
'But leave her praise . . .' intended to follow the superb
hymn that ends with the 'blossoms of pride' line.

The chaotic syntax must often be the mark of an unfinished poem. Every reader will find passages where sentences are left hanging in the air, verbs without subjects,
subjects without verbs, relative clauses with no possible
antecedents, all of which can only be loose ends.

Again, there are images which do not obey the rules
of decorum and logical aptness that Ralegh normally
adheres to so excellently. For example, lines 132–3
are unrelated, the quatrains before and after being
complete:

> And as the icicles in a winter's day   132
>   When as the sun shines with unwonted warm,
> So did my joys melt into secret tears,
>   So did my heart dissolve in wasting drops

He is speaking of earlier and slighter miseries caused by
Cynthia's frowns and goes on to compare his later and
greater despair to the floods that come from the melting

of great snows. Both the sense and the metre in the 'icicles' comparison are incomplete. Does this betoken uneasiness with the image? It involves the suggestion that Ralegh's heart is like an icicle in temperature, and, more important, it relates Cynthia's access of displeasure to the increased _warmth_ of the sun. By contrast and much more fitly, Cynthia's displeasure in line 106 is compared to the _setting_ of the sun. The 'icicles' image may give an exact sensory impression, but it is out of keeping with the needs of the poem; the metrical and grammatical uneasiness probably indicates Ralegh's dissatisfaction. The marks in the manuscript against line 132 presumably indicate that something was to be changed.

Finally, there is the whole question of tone and mood. We have just seen Ralegh making modifications in the poem: I am sure there would have been many more before the poem would have been submitted to the affronted Queen. Just as he tempers the sulks and grumbles in producing the finished version of the 'Petition to Queen Anne', so, I think, the strident emotion of some parts of the _Cynthia_ Book, would have been toned down.

If we accept the suggestion that the poem is unfinished, we must clearly make reservations in our criticism, bearing in mind that we have before us poetry being created, and not a finally completed work of art.

The reader will often find himself baffled by the _general_ obscurity of _Cynthia_ (as opposed to incidental obscurities in the sense). We are left very much in the dark about the course of the relationship Ralegh is talking about; there is an entire absence of clear external references, and many allusions to incidents in the 'love' between Cynthia and the Ocean, which are clearly important, are left quite unexplained. Although undoubtedly the air of mystery which hangs over the whole poem tends to lower its value for us, it is no good blaming Ralegh for a failure of communication. The poem was intended for Elizabeth to see, and perhaps for Ralegh's most intimate circle. They would have had no difficulty in understanding what all the poem was about. We are eavesdroppers and have no right to grumble if we cannot follow the conversation of those we overhear. As communication, *The Ocean to Cynthia* does not need to be clearer to the general public than a private letter is. Ralegh is not guilty of deliberate mystification.

It will also be a fault to expect that the emotions and sentiments described in the poem will necessarily be those experienced by Ralegh in 'real life'. The poem is an appeal for restoration; it is the presentation of a case, a piece of oratory designed to make a queen relent. The desire for self-revelation, the wish to portray feelings accurately, do not inspire the poem. Indeed, the literal truth about Ralegh's feelings need not come into the poem at all: he is not in a court of law, and he may flatter and exaggerate as he likes. More important still, what Ralegh says is governed by certain conventions of poetic address.

First among these conventions is the praise of the Queen. The story of the poets' hymning of Elizabeth is an astonishing one[1] and the reader of Elizabethan poetry who cannot forget the actual figure of the ageing and capricious Queen or who seeks for what is sometimes too narrowly called 'sincerity' is likely to find himself thoroughly bewildered. The Queen is a beautiful virgin, the object of every poet's passion; she is a goddess to be worshipped, the ideal of beauty and chastity, a queen

[1] See E. C. Wilson, *England's Eliza* (1939).

of shepherdesses to be courted, she is the sun and the moon. The reasons for worshipping the virgin queen like this are not simple. Partly, there is the simple flattery by the poet who seeks advancement. Then, in an age which saw in a monarch a representative of God upon earth, a being raised by nature above other beings as the sun was raised above the stars, there was a natural tendency towards a more devout kind of compliment to royalty than we think fitting now (although we can see debased forms of the attitude in the glorification of dictators). Again, we must not forget how sincere was the devotion and gratitude of Englishmen to a queen they recognised to be above the ordinary greatness of monarchs. Finally—and of course, perhaps simultaneously with all these—the hymning of this woman who was queen and virgin was also the hymning of perfection. Royalty and chastity were mystical conditions, and Elizabeth becomes their symbol: a poem about Elizabeth slides easily into a discussion of abstractions. To an age that moved comfortably in the realms of allegory, 'translatio', emblem and symbol, the virgin queen becomes a convenient focussing-point for abstract discussions of love, chastity, piety or beauty—and in a Protestant country almost takes the place of the Blessed Virgin.

'Nowhere,' writes E. C. Wilson, 'is there such a subtle blending of all these types of idealisation and motives for praise as the fragment of Ralegh's *Cynthia* reveals.' The language Ralegh uses about the qualities of Cynthia is not used on oath: it is rhapsodic utterance in a conventional and accepted mode.

There is another, rather thin, garment of 'other-speaking' in the use in the poem of the pastoral convention. Although shepherds and their flocks do not crowd the poem, the allegorical note is enough to make

the personalities of the poem—the poet and his queen—
less particular: the pastoral always *generalises*.

Next, the poem is concerned with the passion of
sexual love: a lover speaks about his former mistress,
about his attraction to her, the bliss of affection returned,
the misery of the loss of love. In all this, the poem bears
no relation to fact. There have been those who have
explained the intimacy between Queen and courtier on
sexual grounds, but they have no shred of evidence.
Ralegh's *real* emotions were those of the courtier who
had enjoyed the favours of his Queen and then had forfeited them: the emotion he describes is that of the dis-
appointed lover. It should also be noted that Ralegh
takes the language of the love he describes from the
medieval convention of 'courtly love', the code origina-
ting with the troubadours. Ralegh is a humble vassal
like all the lovers in 'amour courtois'; he worships his
mistress, who is so far above him, in humility and silence.
She is great and powerful, perfect in mind and beauty;
the lover is willing to undertake the most arduous tasks
that can be imposed upon him and, however disdainful
his mistress may be, he remains unswervingly faithful.
We are at least two removes from the pangs Ralegh
actually suffered, when we read of the course of his
'love'.

As a poem, then, which shares every tendency to
hyperbole found in poetic addresses to Queen Elizabeth;
which talks about a love that never existed and borrows
its notion of love from a poetic convention; which is
designed in the first place to move pity rather than to
speak truth; it may well seem that *The Ocean to Cynthia* is
a piece of vast hypocrisy and rodomontade. Actually, the
successful translation of emotions into accepted conventions does not make the poem less 'genuine'. So far

as its main aim was concerned, Elizabeth and Ralegh's hearers would have applauded the transmutation, and they could easily read the 'key' to the underlying truth. And we, who read the poem at this distance of time, can see that in idealising rather than saying 'this is just how I feel', Ralegh has raised his poem from the introspection of a particular individual to a level where his words can be generally interesting. Step by step we are removed from the private worries of Sir Walter Ralegh, lately relieved of his duties as Captain of the Guard and imprisoned in the Tower, and we almost forget, as we read the poem, that he and Elizabeth of England ever existed. *The Ocean to Cynthia* is important to us because it contains, irrespective of who wrote it, a most moving account of the state of deprivation, a profound analysis (for all the conventions) of the power and nature of love and a comment on mutability that is too impressive to be ignored.

Commentary

Since the poem is very hard to follow, I make no apology for commenting on it at some length. From the start, we are plunged into a kind of waste-land of the spirit. Mr. T. S. Eliot's waste land is a very different thing from Ralegh's, but it is interesting to note the similarities in the images the two poets use to convey the sense of aridity and sterility. Both poets use juxtaposition: Eliot has his lilacs in the dead land, Ralegh his fair flowers amid the brinish sand. There are broken images in Eliot to go with Ralegh's broken monuments; Eliot's dead tree gives no shelter; Ralegh sits alone under 'healthless' trees. Both make rich use of the image of dust, and both find twilight a useful image for the same kind of mood—Eliot has his

> violet hour, the evening hour that strives
> Homeward, and brings the sailor home from sea,
> The typist home at teatime . . .

Ralegh's setting is

> when after Phoebus is descended
> And leaves a light much like the past day's dawning,
> And every toil and labour wholly ended,
> Each living creature draweth to his resting . . .

Even the theme of the withholding of the life-giving waters is used by Ralegh.

The poem opens with death; the verse moves sombrely and slowly to speak of the death of the poet's joys and the death of the mind that must speak of those joys. So numbed is he by sorrows, that he cannot, as he would wish, use 'sweeter words' and 'more becoming verse'. This is the well-known rhetorical device of disclaiming rhetoric—here for the purpose of magnifying the effect of his grief. In fact, of course, the simple words which he pretends are all he can muster are absolutely right and becoming. What could be more effective than the plainness of

> Joys under dust, that never live again?

It suggests irrevocability as more elaborate phrasing would not. The same power is in the heavy monosyllabic tread of

> As to the dead, the dead did these unfold.

where the repeated 'd' gives a strange funeral-march air. Absolute simplicity marks the opening lines ('The idea but resting of a wasted mind' is the only sophisticated line); the images too are very plain: dust, wounds, hearse, fallen blossoms, the cinders of extinguished fires.

The hint of 'the blossoms fallen, the sap gone from the tree' is taken up and developed in the next section (16–36), when the poet amplifies the description of his death-like condition by contrasting it with the happiness he has been deprived of. Past bounty and present dearth are emphasised by a string of 'nature' images, fecundity and sterility being flung together in a series of antitheses. As, for example, in

> Lost in the mud of those high-flowing streams

> All in the shade even in the fair sun days

At times the antithetical balance is elaborate:

> From fruitful trees I gather withered leaves
> And glean the broken ears with miser's hands,
> Who sometime did enjoy the weighty sheaves—
> I seek fair flowers amid the brinish sand.

Here the first and last lines repeat the 'bounty-dearth' antithesis, and between these are two lines each of which expresses a half of the antithesis.

With line 37 the poem turns suddenly and startlingly from loss and despair to a hymn of adoration to Cynthia (the cause of his despair), a hymn that invokes the aid of the rhetorical high style he had so shortly before denounced. This unannounced and radical switch in the thought and mood of the poem is not carelessness: the effect is powerful and was presumably studied. We see the conflict and confusion in the mind of the sufferer—though rejected and cast down and desolate, he is still filled with thoughts of the greatness of the creature who loved him and the greatness of their mutual passion. This greatness has power to fire him even in his distress. There is also irony; to be so carried away by ecstasy increases the pathos when we know his forlorn state:

Ralegh in his later years

The symbolic title page of *The History of the World*

'Whom Love defends, what fortune overthrows?' he cries unthinkingly. Finally, this illogical new direction gives the poem the effect it is meant to give, of a solitary musing, where the thoughts succeed each other not as in rational discourse, but as in day-dreams.

The poet goes on to recall in general terms the blessed days of Cynthia's favour, when she inspired his every action. So he is led to recall one particular instance which I quote not only for a biographical interest, but also because the passage excellently illustrates the difficulty of parts of the poem:

> The honour of her love, love still devising,
>   Wounding my mind with contrary conceit,
> Transferred itself sometime to her aspiring,
>   Sometime the trumpet of her thought's retreat;
> To seek new worlds, for gold, for praise, for glory,
>   To try desire, to try love severed far,
> When I was gone she sent her memory
>   More strong than were ten thousand ships of war
> To call me back, to leave great honour's thought,
>   To leave my friends, my fortune, my attempt,
> To leave the purpose I so long had sought,
>   And hold both cares and comforts in contempt.

The next section of the poem (69–103) again begins very abruptly with no bridge from the preceding section, and this time the abruptness has no special virtue. This whole section is one long sentence building up by simile on simile to a climax, and is an excellent example of the 'cumulative' power of Ralegh's verse. The poet explains that love cannot suddenly cease to be, there is an impetus which carries it on even after the death-blow has been given; he tells how, his energy deserting him, he is trying to hold fast to the dying passion and enshrine it in verse before it is a nothingness. He compares this growing

I

numbness to a 'body violently slain' which 'retaineth warmth although the spirit be gone', to the earth deserted by the summer sun, 'producing some green, though not as it hath done', and to a millwheel, 'forced by the falling stream', which

> Although the course be turned some other way
> Doth for a time go round upon the beam,
> Till wanting strength to move, it stands at stay.

The great image of twilight closes the story of him who

> Alone, forsaken, friendless on the shore,
> With many wounds, with death's cold pangs embraced,
> Writes in the dust as one that could no more,
> Whom love and time and fortune had defaced,
> Of things so great, so long, so manifold,
> With means so weak (the soul even then departing)—
> The weal, the woe, the passages of old
> And worlds of thought described by one last sighing;
> As if when after Phoebus is descended
> And leaves a light much like the past day's dawning,
> And every toil and labour wholly ended
> Each living creature draweth to his resting,
> We should begin, by such a parting light,
> To write the story of all ages past
> And end the same before th'approaching night.

(Part of the appeal of these last lines is adventitious: we cannot help looking to the time ahead when Ralegh does really begin to write 'the story of all ages past' in the gathering gloom of his last years in the Tower.)

All the images in this long sentence are rich in suggestion. Not only do they convey the notion of the gradual cessation of motive power or spirit, but they also help to illustrate other aspects of the poet's condition. The body has been violently slain as Ralegh's happiness was violently curtailed; the earth, 'in cold winter days' deserted by the 'life-giving sun', brings in nature imagery once more to describe the sterility of his spirit, and the image also equates the Queen with the sun; the turning away of the life-giving water of love is implied in the image of the diverted mill-stream; the twilight image again brings in the sun-queen parallel. The lower layers of parallelism in these images are not recondite: Ralegh always makes it easy for the reader to grasp not only the leading purpose of an image but the subsidiary purposes also.

The next few stanzas continue to describe his past love: absence could never lessen its force. With line 120 it may appear that a connected narrative is about to commence:

> Twelve years entire I wasted in this war,
>   Twelve years of my most happy younger days,
> But I in them, and they now wasted are—
>   Of all which past the sorrow only stays.

But this poem never starts: it is always about to relate the whole great tragedy, but then is pulled aside into a digression. Then we reach a point at which we realise that the whole story has, piecemeal, been related and there is nothing more to do except bring the poem to a close. So here the last line of the quatrain, quoted from an earlier poem, recalls the occasion of writing that poem, and Ralegh turns aside to dwell on that past anticipation of present misery; this digression leads him on to an entirely new subject, and thus capriciously the meditation pursues its unpredictable course.

Lines 143–173 are a moving description of the first reactions of the poet to being dismissed by Cynthia. 'Furious madness where true reason lacked' gave way to settled misery as he strove to cast out from his heart his love for the woman who had so cruelly served him:

And as a man distract, with treble might,
Bound in strong chains, doth strive and rage in vain
  Till, tired and breathless, he is forced to rest,
Finds by contention but increase of pain
  And fiery heat inflamed in swollen breast,
So did my mind in change of passion
  From woe to wrath, from wrath return to woe,
Struggling in vain from love's subjection.

. . . . . .

I hated life and cursed destiny,
  The thoughts of passed times like flames of hell
Kindled afresh within my memory
  The many dear achievements that befell
In those prime years and infancy of love,
  Which to describe were but to die in writing.

This section ends with a 'signpost' pointing forward to the theme of unremoving, unalterable devotion (implied in the rhapsodies to Cynthia already sung). He could not banish his affection:

Ah, those I sought but vainly to remove,
  And vainly shall, by which I perish living.

He reminds himself (173–180) that reason, holding before his eyes the transitoriness of all earthly things, should have warned him that passion must decay as beauty decays—but what has Time to do with the timelessness of his passion or the divinity of Cynthia? His verse swings into the rhythm of one of those ascending chants of praise he excels in:

A beauty that can easily deceive
  Th' arrest of years, and creeping age outclimb,
A spring of beauties which time ripeth not—
  Time that but works on frail mortality—
A sweetness which woe's wrongs outwipeth not,
  Whom love hath chose for his divinity,

> A vestal fire that burns but never wasteth,
>> That looseth naught by giving light to all,
> That endless shines each where and endless lasteth,
>> Blossoms of pride that can nor fade nor fall.

The image of the 'vestal fire' is rich and lovely; it suggests worship of a goddess, the virginity of Elizabeth, and light which shines with undiminished brightness, though shared out to all, brings in once more the suggestion of the sun. The stanzas which follow this passage, I have already discussed (pp. 104–5), suggesting that they are not fully worked into the poem.

The next section (221–298), containing some of the finest writing in the poem, is an odd amalgam of generalised statement on the nature of love with some obviously personal reminiscences. Line 219 is the keynote:

> In love those things that were, no more may be.

He starts with an elaborate comparison: love is like a dammed-up river:

>> a stream by strong hand bounded in
>> From nature's course.

But this artificial lake, finding a small rent in the bank, makes a channel for itself and then bursts out into its old course as a river, blotting out the work of years in a moment:

>> Such is of women's love the careful charge,
> Held and maintained with multitude of woes—
>> Of long erections such the sudden fall;
> One hour diverts, one instant overthrows,
>> For which our lives, for which our fortune's thrall,
> So many years those joys have dearly bought,
>> Of which when our fond hopes do most assure,
> All is dissolved, our labours come to naught,
>> Nor any mark thereof there doth endure.

There is a great bitterness in these lines and those following, which tell how past achievements and service do him no good now, but there also emerges a thought which takes the edge off the bitterness. To dam a stream is to go against 'nature's course'; like a stream, love can never be still but would always be flowing; it is *unnatural* to try to hold it fast. For a moment the poet accepts the necessity of change. Underlying his misery is the recognition that love must change and pass on, since nothing in nature stays fixed and immutable:

> All droops, all dies, all trodden under dust.

By the use of images of the seasonal death of fruit and flower, he suggests a feeling of acquiescence with the inevitable rhythm of birth, growth and death in time:

> As Time gave, Time did again devour.

So he finds consolation, that the passing of love is like the passing of all things. Because of this sense of inevitability, his very gloomiest sentences take on a light that makes them more affirmations than denials:

> With youth is dead the hope of love's return,
> Who looks not back to hear our after cries.

If anyone is to blame, it is himself for thinking to build on a happiness he should have known must decay.

And yet—and yet! 'I powerless was to alter my desire', 'my love is *not of time*'. The poet's love, *his* affection, is unchanging. True love, such as he feels, in spite of the suffering it brings, is yet the quintessence of existence, that which purifies and gives meaning to our lives. Shared affection may decay in time, but real devotion like his endures through all. His revenge for Cynthia's betrayal could not be hate, for love is not love that alters when it alteration finds:

Erring or never erring, such is love,
　　As while it lasteth scorns the accompt of those
Seeking but self contentment to improve.

From line 318, such is the turmoil of the thought—
whether intentional or not—that it is hard to make useful
divisions of the poem into sections any further. A certain self-pity creeps in (319–326): in spite of this long
and great passion, Cynthia has been as severe as a
stranger. What is the point of complaining? the damage
is done:

　　The limbs divided, sundered and a-bleeding
　　　　Cannot complain the sentence was uneven.

Lines 344–349 are a hymn of adoration to Cynthia,
apparently taken from an earlier part of *Cynthia* ('Such
didst thou her long since describe, yet sighing'), repeated
here with some sarcasm. And he adds:

　　But what hath it availed thee so to write?
　　She cares not for thy praise, who knows not theirs,
　　　　It's now an idle labour and a tale
　　Told out of tune that dulls the hearers' ears.

He continues complaining of Cynthia's injustice until line
376, when there is another of those sudden changes of
mood. The poem has been quietening down, the
anguish turning to lethargic melancholy. Now, with the
sudden:

　　Yet greater fancy beauty never bred

the smouldering fire blazes again. From being querulous,
he takes wing on the memory of the greatness of her he
loved, the greatness of their mutual passion and the
undeviating fidelity of his own affection:

> A love obscured but cannot be forgotten,
>   Too great and strong for Time's jaws to devour
>   .   .   .   .   .
>   These thoughts, knit up by faith, shall ever last,
>   These, Time assays, but never can untie.

The sustained flow of the poem from 376–415 is really most compelling. Nothing 'can so dissolve, dissever or destroy The essential love', the memories will always be with him:

>   and remain
>   Of my sad heart the sorrow-sucking bees.

Lines 416–461 continue to explore the quality of this love that causes suffering and at the same time gives a meaning to life. Dull sublunary lovers' love would have ceased with the wrongs he has received, for the objective of their love is only delight; it

>   Stays by the pleasure but no longer stays.

But his love has a spiritual quality:

> But in my mind so is her love enclosed
>   And is thereof not only the best part
> But into it the essence is disposed . . .
>   O love (the more my woe), to it thou art
> Even as the moisture in each plant that grows,
>   Even as the sun unto the frozen ground,
> Even as the sweetness to th' incarnate rose,
>   Even as the centre in each perfect round,
> As water to the fish, to men as air,
>   As heat to fire, as light unto the sun—
> O love! it is but vain to say 'thou were',
>   Ages and times cannot thy power outrun:
> Thou art the soul of that unhappy mind
>   Which, being by nature made an idle thought,
> Began even then to take immortal kind
>   When first her virtues in thy spirits wrought.

> From thee, therefore, that mover cannot move,
>   Because it is become thy cause of being.

His love is at the centre of his heart 'till all break and all
dissolve to dust'—even if it at times is like a poisoned
arrow, eating away his earthly happiness. The justification of this paradox that love both wounds and gives life
is an imaginative one that poetry and not exegesis can
express.

This wave of idealistic excitement breaks suddenly.
He stops short with a gesture of despair:

> But what of those, or these, or what of aught
>   Of that which was, or that which is, to treat?

The broken rhythm of the lines well impresses on the
reader the sudden disappearance of the motive force
which has driven the poetry along in the previous 80
lines. The speaker continues with the bitterest lines,
a cynicism the more bitter as the immediately preceding
idealism has been ecstatic:

> What I possess is but the same I sought,
>   My love was false, my labours were deceit.
> No less than such they are esteemed to be—
>   A fraud bought at the price of many woes,
> A guile, whereof the profits unto me—
>   Could it be thought premeditate for those?

He is suggesting, though the last line suggests incredulity,
that happiness in love is always a will-o'-the-wisp.

After these two extremes of idealism and bitterness,
the poem finds its equilibrium in a kind of exhaustion of
passion, a mood of defeated resignation (474). The
verse moves with a sad dignity to:

> On Sestus shore, Leander's late resort,
>   Hero hath left no lamp to guide her love,

and the mournfulness brings the poetry almost to a dead stop in the middle of a line:

> She is gone, she is lost . . . . .

But the very finality of the words quicken him to rebellion and he denies them as soon as he utters them, and the line becomes a strange presentation of the whole paradox of this strange poem:

> She is gone, she is lost—She is found, she is ever fair!
>   Sorrow draws weakly where love draws not too;
> Woe's cries sound nothing but only in love's ear—
>   Do then by dying what life cannot do.

Some have taken this as the turning point of the whole poem, but it is not so. His denial is a momentary, irresistible ejaculation, expressing the division in his mind that has been present throughout the poem. A coal glows white hot and then dies to an ember and the poem continues with the settled unhappiness that had preceded the outburst. The important *addition* to the poem (not change) which the cry makes lies in the line, 'Do then by dying what life cannot do.' His love still exists, but its object is no longer found perfectly in the woman who has been inconstant; although the earthly love was necessary, although it enables his spirit 'to take immortal kind', it does not provide lasting satisfaction and fulfilment; he will not find that fulfilment now until after death. The poet was talking about death before the interruption of 'She is found, she is ever fair!', and as he resumes the theme, death becomes not only the relief from suffering it had been but also an aspiration to unqualified joy. 'She is found' does not mean that Cynthia has relented; it means the image he once found and fixed his devotion to in Cynthia is still present—but not in

Cynthia or in any earthly woman—'Do then by dying what life cannot do.'

In the closing stanzas there is a fine dignity:

> Unfold thy flocks and leave them to the fields
> To feed on hills or dales where likes them best
> Of what the summer or the spring-time yields,
> For love and time hath given thee leave to rest.
>
> .   .   .   .
>
> Thus home I draw as death's long night draws on,
> Yet every foot, old thoughts turn back mine eyes.

The deeply-moving conclusion starts with affirmation and ends in perplexity:

> To God I leave it, who first gave it me
>   And I her gave, and she returned again
> As it was hers. So let His mercies be
>   Of my last comforts the essential mean.
>   But be it so or not, th' effects are past:
>   Her love hath end, my woe must ever last.

It is far better that Ralegh ends his extraordinary poem with a gesture of helplessness than an affirmation—say, of the neo-platonic idea expressed or hinted at in 'Do then by dying what life cannot do.' For it was not the purpose of his poetry to present tidy systems and neat philosophical answers to the problems of existence. He presents paradoxes, and hints at their solutions. *Cynthia* is one vast paradox—so paradoxical at times that it almost degenerates into muddle. He both loves and hates; love brought and brings both sorrow and joy; love dies, love does not die; it was at least worth loving, it was folly ever to have loved; he tries hard to find some solution, lights on the possibility of a woman's love being a preparation for a higher love—but that does not lessen the bitterness. What other conclusion can there be other than the simple expression of fact?

> Her love hath end, my woe must ever last.

An important footnote to *Cynthia* is the fragment of the next Book, 'entreating of Sorrow', which follows on in the Hatfield Manuscript. It runs to only $21\frac{1}{2}$ lines, in tercets, and consists of a short statement of the poet's woe followed by an elaborate image. It is the image that is important. The poet is abandoned by Cynthia and others have taken his place in her affection. In this rejection and new-gathering, Cynthia is like the sun, which nurtures young growing things, then leaves them to die while it fosters a new brood, its own power remaining constant and unaffected by the succession of growth it both observes and causes. Cynthia is, then, the sun:

> Which sees the burial and birth of all else,
> And holds that power with which she first begun:

> Leaving each withered body to be torn
>   By fortune and by times tempestuous,
> Which by her virtue, once fair fruit have born,

> Knowing she can renew and can create
>   Green from the ground and flowers even out of stone
> By virtue lasting over time and date . . .

The analogy of sun and monarch is, of course, traditional. From one aspect, this image is a 'praise' of Queen Elizabeth and exalts her power and brilliance. The power that is talked of is not, however, merely the life-giving power. With greater realism than is often found among those who address their sovereign, Ralegh extends the comparison, and attributes to Elizabeth that part of the cycle of the sun's activity which causes death in the living organism after it has been brought up to maturity and fruition. In *Cynthia* Ralegh many times used the image of the sunset or winter to describe the withdrawing of the Queen's favour. But they were particular images for particular purposes. Here the whole cycle of birth, growth and decay—of acceptance, favour and rejection—is attributed to Elizabeth as a necessary quality of her power. She must create, she must destroy, she must then create new things. And the importance of the vision is this. In *Cynthia* there was conflict in the poet's mind between Cynthia as divine, beneficent, life-giving perfection and Cynthia as a cruel woman, discarding those whom she had loved as fickle women do. But now this discarding is seen as a vital part of her sun-like, superhuman nature. She *is* all-great and life-giving, like the sun; she is still all-great when she destroys and takes new creatures to foster. Ralegh affirms what he was at one point working towards in *Cynthia*, that the mutability of the Queen's affection is part of the mutability of all things growing on earth. But he is able also still to retain the feeling of the Queen's omnipotence. Without feeling any the less misery for his having been abandoned, he can see abandonment as part of an inevitable process of change which must be acquiesced in, since it is the governing principle of continuance in life. Of course, if one looks too literally at the notion, it is absurd in that the supersession of Ralegh by Essex in Elizabeth's favour has nothing to do with the continuance of England. But it has already been pointed out that literalism hardly enters into poems about the Queen; we must be prepared to accept higher and abstract imaginative levels. Ralegh comes to recognise a necessary mutability in human relations; though he suffers, he must not repine—there is some order and meaning in the cycle of change. There is a faint tinge of the consolation for suffering that is found in tragedy. It is perhaps this consolation that Ralegh means in the strange image with which the poem breaks off:

> Leaving us only woe which, like the moss
>   Having compassion of unburied bones,
> Cleaves to mischance and unrepaired loss.

> For tender stalks . . .

Chapter Four

THE PROSE

THE profuseness and variety of Ralegh's prose writings are formidable. As a naval commander, he sends an excited account of a great battle to a friend; for his son he inscribes some rather heavy-handed paternal advice; he translates excerpts from a Sceptic philosopher; he extols the virtues of Guiana as a colony; he composes a treatise on the art of war at sea; from the Tower he gives a monarch advice on the disposing of his children in marriage, writes a tract on parliamentary government, and over the long years sets forth his sombre philosophy of history in his story of man from his beginnings to the days of the Roman Empire. The reader may well be daunted by such diversity of material, much of it written for occasions and purposes that have now no interest, much of it fragmentary, and some of it, alas, very dull. The prose is not very accessible, either, to the general reader: the last edition of the Works was in 1829, and the selections from the prose that are available suffer from the disadvantages of all anthologies. The purpose of this chapter is to sort out for the reader, with the help of liberal quotation, what is important and valuable among the mass of Ralegh's writings in prose.

I shall not exhibit strings of passages as particularly fine specimens of English prose-style: a collocation of eloquent paragraphs set down for the reader to admire would be as useless as the detached 'beauties' of Shakespeare. In prose as in verse, it is vain to consider style as a thing in itself. Form depends on function, and how good the form, or style, of a passage is, cannot be judged until we take the whole work into account, examine its aim and intention and see what part the passage plays in fulfilling that aim. I shall concern myself with what Ralegh has to say and how effectively he says it.

In the first place, Ralegh's prose must be divided into two kinds: the prose of action, and the prose of reflection. Within these two divisions will be found many different types of writing, answering the needs of particular works, but this first separation is fundamental.

The Prose of Action

The prose of action comprises accounts of actions or exploits in which Ralegh took part or had a particular interest. This type of literature is one we know well enough today, but Ralegh's reasons for writing were generally very different from the reasons of those who today publish stories of personal adventure and unusual excitements. Ralegh never thought of the writing-up of his actions as a 'literary' endeavour or an attempt to make capital from the public's desire for vicarious adventure— nor did he undertake exploits in order to write books about them. Some of his 'prose of action', for example, is embedded in his historical writing, where it serves for illustration and comparison; accounts of his last fatal expedition were written as memoranda or private letters in his own justification; the *Discovery of Guiana* was written to enlist approval and support for a colonial scheme.

The earliest piece is Ralegh's first published work in prose and concerns an action in which he took no part: *A Report of the Truth of the Fight about the Isles of Azores this last Summer, Betwixt the Revenge, one of Her Majesty's Ships, and an Armada of the King of Spain* (1591). To appreciate how good this account of Grenville's heroic foolhardiness is, the reader should turn, after sampling it, to the ballad which Ralegh's account inspired Tennyson to write on the subject. Tennyson, substituting a rather jaunty bravado for the spirit that moves Ralegh, and writing up the story in verse, loses the ready appeal which Ralegh's direct and unadorned relation has. Ralegh's heart and style go together; both heart and style are a little uneasy in Tennyson, and they are out of step. Ralegh knows that the tale of Grenville's astonishing 'greatness of heart' in defying impossible odds is so impressive that the deeds are best left to speak for themselves, with as little elaboration and indirection as possible.[1]

The spirit behind the work is, like the style, simple and without subtlety. Ralegh is moved by admiring wonder at a course of action quite impolitic and inexpedient, foredoomed to failure, which, because it humiliated an arrogant and evil enemy, deserved to be called not folly but heroism. Ralegh loves Grenville's courage and resolution 'never to submit or yield' in a cause sanctified as a good cause. The love and wonder make his account glow with enthusiasm. 'The other course had been the better', he says—to have got out of the way when the Spanish fleet bore up—'notwithstanding, out of the

[1] In praising the work's 'sane and manly style', Edmund Gosse stated that it marked 'the highest level reached by English narrative prose as it existed before the waters were troubled by the fashion of Euphues' (*Raleigh* (1886) p. 51). But both before and after Euphuism, both 'sane and manly' styles and highly ornate styles can be found in abundance, often in the same writer; the arbiter, always, is not the year in which the work is written, but the purpose for which it was written. For narratives of action, a direct, simple and vigorous style is the rule rather than the exception throughout the period from 1590 until Ralegh's death.

greatness of his mind, he could not be persuaded.' Ralegh tells quickly and vividly how the little English fleet was caught at anchor and unready, the ships' companies halved by disease and many men ashore; how Grenville in the *Revenge* 'utterly refusing to turn from the enemy' sailed into the midst of the two Spanish squadrons; how he was laid aboard by ship after ship in turn, but fought them all off, inflicting heavy losses, through the afternoon and night until he himself was wounded and his ship had become a hulk, and all that flesh and blood could do to resist had been done.

All the powder of the *Revenge* to the last barrel was now spent, all her pikes broken, forty of her best men slain and the most part of the rest hurt. In the beginning of the fight she had but one hundred free from sickness, and fourscore and ten sick laid in hold upon the ballast. A small troop to man such a ship, and a weak garrison to resist so mighty an army. By those hundred all was sustained, the volleys, boardings and enterings of fifteen ships of war, besides those which beat her at large. On the contrary, the Spanish were always supplied with soldiers brought from every squadron— all manner of arms and powder at will. Unto ours there remained no comfort at all, no hope, no supply either of ships, men or weapons; the masts all beaten overboard, all her tackle cut asunder, her upperwork altogether rased; and in effect evened she was with the water—but the very foundation or bottom of a ship, nothing being left overhead either for flight or defence. Sir Richard finding himself in this distress, and unable any longer to make resistance, having endured in this fifteen hours' fight the assault of fifteen several Armadoes all by turns aboard him . . . and that himself and the ship must needs be possessed by the enemy, who were now all cast in a ring round about him—the *Revenge* not able to move one way or other but as she was moved with the waves and billow of the sea, commanded the

Master Gunner, whom he knew to be a most resolute man,
to split and sink the ship, that thereby nothing might remain
of glory or victory to the Spaniards . . . And persuaded
the company, or as many as he could induce, to yield themselves unto God and to the mercy of none else; but as they
had, like valiant, resolute men, repulsed so many enemies,
they should not now shorten the honour of their nation
by prolonging their own lives for a few hours or a few
days.

The ship's company, however, refused to scuttle and Sir
Richard was taken on board a Spanish ship and honour-
ably treated before he died of his wounds.

The celebration of Grenville's pertinacity and courage
was only a part of Ralegh's purpose in writing his narrative; the pamphlet is also designed as a blow in the anti-
Spanish campaign, in support of Ralegh's policy of aggression. So the action of the *Revenge* is set within an account
of recent happenings in the war and is accompanied
by general reflections on the Spanish menace. Ralegh
reminds his readers with some satisfaction of the fate of
Spanish imperialist designs in 1588, when the invincible
Armada was 'driven with squibs from their anchors and
chased out of the sight of England'. Grenville's fight
is a moral victory in the cause so near to Ralegh's heart.
But his hostility to Spain as he here expresses it is not
a jingoistic and truculent one. The emphasis is everywhere on defence against being engulfed by a cruel and
irreligious imperialism rather than on attack against a
rival power. Ralegh's indignation at the barbarities practised by the Spaniards in the Indies and Peru, under the
cloak of spreading faith amongst the heathen, rings with a
sincere and genuine tone.

The other naval action of which Ralegh has left an
account is the engagement at Cadiz (seen by Ralegh as

revenge for the *Revenge*) which has been discussed in
Chapter One. The account, not published in his lifetime,
is given in a letter to an unnamed friend and is born of an
entirely different spirit from the account of the *Revenge*;
the difference is reflected in the markedly different
style. There is a boyish exuberance about it all, like the
zest of a fighter-pilot; the description of how Essex called
out 'Entramos' and 'cast his hat into the sea for joy' is
typical of the mood of the whole. The mood has its
dangers: it may descend into a cocksure bravado, an
unjustified contempt for the enemy and a delight in
battle for its own sake. The only time Ralegh actually
oversteps the mark is at the very end when his lust for
loot and his spite at not being able to satisfy that lust
are very apparent. In general, one is more impressed by
the very real daring and skill that lie behind the racy
narrative.

The letter wonderfully conveys Ralegh's excitement.
Take the unusually vivid images, for example: 'They
hoped to have stumbled the leading ship', 'I was first
saluted by the fort called Philip', 'I bestowed a benediction amongst them', 'I laid out a warp by the side of the
Philip to shake hands with her', 'The Flemings . . . used
merciless slaughter till they were by myself and afterwards by my Lord Admiral beaten off'. The sheer
energy of the account is remarkable. The sense of imme-
diacy and participation is brought to the reader far more
vividly than in most eye-witness narratives, yet Ralegh
is no war-correspondent but a leading participant, fully
and hotly engaged in the business of the battle and concerned in his report only to tell his correspondent just
what happened. Here is an extract from the extraordinary description of the final plight of the Spanish
Galleons:

They all let slip and ran aground, tumbling into the sea heaps of soldiers, so thick as if coals had been poured out of a sack, in many ports at once—some drowned and some sticking in the mud. The *Philip* and the *St. Thomas* burned themselves; the *St. Matthew* and the *St. Andrew* were recovered by our boats ere they could get out to fire them. The spectacle was very lamentable on their side, for many drowned themselves; many, half-burned, leapt into the water; very many hanging by the ropes' ends by the ships' side under the water even to the lips; many, swimming with grievous wounds, strucken under water and put out of their pain; and, withal, so huge a fire, and such tearing of the ordnance in the great *Philip* and the rest when the fire came to them, as if any man had a desire to see Hell itself, it was there most lively figured.

In such a passage, we can see that the thrill of the romance and glory of war is not the whole of Ralegh's attitude and that the utter disenchantment with war which finds expression in *The History of the World* and the *Discourse of the Cause of War* is perhaps born of a very real and personal knowledge of the suffering to the unoffending that is brought by the ambitious schemes of contending States.

Other naval and military adventures of his own, or that he heard from the lips of participants, are scattered about the *History*, where they are used for comment of various kinds—the assault on Fayal during the Islands Voyage (V, 1, ix) illustrating the theory that it is easier to assault a coast than to defend it. These accounts are too fragmentary, however, to be discussed on their own.

There is no doubt that much of the appeal of Ralegh's 'prose of action' for the modern reader is that it gives us an easy entry into the heart of that unique world of Elizabethan maritime adventure—the Armada, Drake, the North-West passage, Hakluyt. Whether or no it is

true that the sea is in the Englishman's blood, *writings*
about the sea are: he thrills all the more to discovery,
exploration and sea-battles when he has not to endure the
hard-lying and scanty fare that inevitably attend them.
Ralegh is a superb dispenser of Elizabethan adventure,
and that without striving for effect. The plain statement
of facts which opens his *Discovery of Guiana* captures the
glamour of voyaging to far-off and little-known lands in a
way an historical novelist might well envy:

> On Thursday the 6 of February in the year 1595, we de-
> parted England, and the Sunday following had sight of the
> north cape of Spain, the wind for the most part continuing
> prosperous; we passed in sight of the Burlings and the Rock,
> and so onwards for the Canaries, and fell with Fuerte Ven-
> tura the 17 of the same month, where we spent two or
> three days and relieved our companies with some fresh meat.
> From thence we coasted by the Gran Canaria, and so to
> Tenerife, and stayed there for the *Lion*'s *Whelp*, your Lord-
> ship's ship, and for Captain Amyas Preston and the rest;
> but when after 7 or 8 days we found them not, we departed
> and directed our course for Trinidado with mine own ship
> and a small barque of Captain Cross's only (for we had
> before lost sight of a small gallego on the coast of Spain
> which came with us from Plymouth). We arrived at
> Trinidado the 22 of March, casting anchor at Point Curiapan,
> which the Spaniards call Punto de Gallo, which is situate in
> 8 degrees or thereabouts; we abode there 4 or 5 days, and in
> all that time we came not to the speech of any Indian or
> Spaniard: on the coast we saw a fire, as we sailed from the
> point Carao towards Curiapan, but for fear of the Spaniards,
> none durst come to speak with us.

What follows is no anti-climax to so promising a beginning. We must, of course, separate the adventitious
interest of the narrative—its power to recreate a world
lost to modern landlubbers—from its real and per-

manent value, but there is no reason why we should not take all the pleasure we can find from its wonderful atmosphere. There is a particular relish, for example, in pioneer researches into anthropology and 'human geography' which brush against men whose heads grow beneath their shoulders. The romance of modern science is of a different kind. An excellent example of the atmosphere of the work is in the account of the meeting with Topiawari, which is worth quoting at some length.

The next day following, before noon, he came to us on foot from his house, which was fourteen English miles (himself being 110 years old) and returned on foot the same day, and with him many of the borderers, with many women and children, that came to wonder at our nation, and to bring us down victual, which they did in great plenty, as venison, pork, hens, chickens, foul, fish, with divers sorts of excellent fruits and roots and great abundance of Pinas, the princess of fruits that grow under the sun, especially those of Guiana. They brought us also store of bread and of their wine, and a sort of Paraquitos no bigger than wrens, and of all other sorts both small and great: one of them gave me a beast called by the Spaniards 'Armadilla', which they call 'Cassacam' . . . somewhat like to a Renocero, with a white horn growing in his hinder parts as big as a great hunting horn, which they use to wind instead of a trumpet. Monardus writeth that a little of the powder of that horn, put into the ear, cureth deafness.

After this old king had rested a while in a little tent that I caused to be set up, I began by my interpreter to discourse with him of the death of Morequito his predecessor, and afterwards of the Spaniards, and, ere I went any further, I made him know the cause of my coming thither, whose servant I was, and that the Queen's pleasure was I should undertake the voyage for their defence and to deliver them from the tyranny of the Spaniards, dilating at large (as I had done before to those of Trinidado) her Majesty's greatness, her justice, her charity to all oppressed nations, with as many of the rest of her beauties and virtues, as either I could express or they conceive, all which being with great admiration attentively heard and marvellously admired, I began to sound the old man as touching Guiana and the state thereof: what sort of commonwealth it was, how governed, of what strength and policy, how far it extended . . . [*he receives his answers*] . . . I asked which nations those were which inhabited on the further side of those mountains, beyond the valley of Amariocapana. He answered with a great sigh (as a man which had inward feeling of the loss of his country and liberty, especially for that his eldest son was slain in a battle on that side of the mountains, whom he most entirely loved) that he remembered in his father's lifetime when he was very old, and himself a young man, that there came down into that large valley of Guiana a nation from so far off as the sun slept (for such were his own words) with so great a multitude as they could not be numbered nor resisted, and that they wore large coats, and hats of crimson colour (which colour he expressed by showing a piece of red wood wherewith my tent was supported) and that they were called Oreiones and Epuremei, those that had slain and rooted out so many of the ancient people as there were leaves in the wood upon all the trees and had now made themselves Lords of all . . .

Although it is true, and Ralegh excuses himself for it, that he has 'neither studied phrase, form nor fashion', *The Discovery of Guiana* is not simply a straightforward journal of events. He wanted to advertise the virtues of Guiana as a colony, and blended with direct description are passages of deliberate eloquence painting as attractive a picture as possible to the English reader who might have capital for investment. The 'earthly-paradise' passages (see p. 18) are very skilfully done and are a tribute to Ralegh's art rather than to the unconscious poetry in the soul of an explorer. However, the work stands by the freshness and vividness of its reporting rather than by Ralegh's powers of persuasion; it is in fact because it is a travel book without the literary vices of most travel books that it is so fine a literary work. The images have the spontaneity of a gay fancy: 'flowers and trees of that variety as were sufficient to make ten volumes of herbals'; along the river where tribes lived in tree-houses his boat grounded 'and stuck so fast as we thought that even there our discovery had ended and we must have left sixty of our men to have inhabited like rooks upon trees with those nations'; the marvellous crystal mountain was like 'a white church tower of exceeding height' and the torrent that dashed down it 'falleth to the ground with a terrible noise and clamour, as if a thousand great bells were knocked one against another'.

It is pathetic indeed to turn from the optimistic and eager narrative of the promise of Guiana to the wretchedness of Ralegh's various accounts of the utter failure of the 1618 expedition (which have already been discussed in Chapter One). Here is different prose indeed; at times strained, hectic and disordered, but at times of great nobility, when Ralegh's spirit rises in passion against the injustice he has received, or when, in the simplest words, despair records despair (see p. 39). The *Apology* for his voyage is of course not at all in the same category with other 'prose of action' since it is less an account than an argument in self-justification. Though the language stutters at times with indignation and bitterness, it has its own distinction: Ralegh was almost incapable of writing badly. Is it so strange, he writes, that he should have failed in his enterprise 'being but a private man and drawing after me the chains and fetters wherewith I had been thirteen years tied in the Tower'?

The long-drawn-out cadences carry the sense onwards though syntax is lost in the eagerness with which he writes:

> A strange fancy had it been in me to have persuaded my son, whom I have lost, and to have persuaded my wife to have adventured the eight thousand pounds which His Majesty gave them for Sherborne, and when that was spent to persuade her to sell her house at Mitcham, in hope of enriching them by the mines of Guiana, if I myself had not seen them with my own eyes; for being old and sickly, thirteen years in prison and not used to the air, to travail and to watching, it being ten to one that I should ever have returned, and of which by reason of my violent sickness and the long continuance thereof no man had any hope, what madness would have made me undertake this journey, but the assurance of the mine?

The Prose of Reflection

The miscellaneous works of 'reflection' are an arid field: they do not increase our respect for Ralegh as a writer or a thinker though they show the breadth of his interests. The political writings are tedious, derivative and inconsistent. *The Prince or Maxims of State* and *The Cabinet Council* (the manuscript of which came into the hands of Milton, who published it) cannot be considered as original writings, so heavily do they rely on other authors,[1] and as both the matter and the manner are uninteresting they may be left to the specialist in Renaissance political theory and the influence of Machiavelli on English thought. A more lively piece of political theory is *The Prerogative of Parliaments in England*, written during Ralegh's last years in the Tower and addressed to the

[1] See Laurence Stapleton, 'Halifax and Raleigh', *Journal of the History of Ideas*, ii (1941), pp. 211–224.

King. Framed as a dialogue between a Counsellor of State and a Justice of the Peace, its retailing of constitutional history is enlivened by the disagreement of the protagonists and sharpened by the contemporary references and anecdotes which Ralegh intersperses. Ralegh has been attacked for being too much on the side of absolute monarchy, and Stebbing quite rightly defends him on the grounds that a Tudor courtier could not help looking at the monarchy with different eyes from those of the Long Parliament. He points out that Ralegh's tract was actually written to persuade the King to call a Parliament, and was far too much to the 'left' in tone for the pleasure of James's court. It is the Justice of the Peace who is given the better of the argument all along, as he defends the acts of Parliament throughout its history, sticks up for its rights and assures his opponent that Crown and Parliament are each other's helpmeets rather than antagonists. A note of adulation and deference to the King and his rights it would be extraordinary not to find in a work of persuasion addressed to His Majesty: Ralegh's candid opinion of monarchs can be seen in *The History of the World* where tact and diplomacy do not inhibit him as they do here—as when for example the Justice warns the Counsellor not to 'dig out of the dust the long-buried memory of the subjects' former contentions with the King'. 'What mean you by that?' asks the Counsellor. 'I will tell your Lordship when I dare', comes the answer. It is worth mentioning in passing that this work shows a far greater understanding of the dynamics of social and political change than all the pieces Ralegh translated from Italian theorists: 'The wisdom of our own age is the foolishness of another: the time present ought not to be referred[1] to the policy that was

---

[1] Surely this, and not the 'preferred' of the text is the right reading?

but the policy that was to the time present: so that the power of the nobility being now withered and the power of the people in the flower, the care to content them would not be neglected.'

The style of the work calls for little comment: there is considerable variety, from the colloquial exchanges like this, on Richard II:

> Yet you see he was deposed by Parliament.

> As well may your Lordship say he was knocked on the head by Parliament,

to such heavy Old Testament rhythms as in:

> Nay, my Lord, so many other goodly manors have passed from His Majesty as the very heart of the kingdom mourneth to remember it, and the eyes of the kingdom shed tears continually at the beholding it: Yea, the soul of the kingdom is heavy unto death with the consideration thereof.

Other advice that the King received from his temerarious prisoner related to the proposed double match of Prince Henry and his sister with a princess and prince of the House of Savoy. Though Ralegh is always deferential when he speaks directly to James, the tone of the whole is very much man-to-man, and some of the implications are not exactly discreet, as, for example, when he speaks in disgust of the callousness of Kings in using their children as pawns in political chess. Both tracts—Ralegh wrote one opposing each of the two suggested marriages —are readable and convincing. Ralegh demonstrates the impolicy and uselessness of any alliance with Savoy, and hostility to Spain is the leit-motiv of his song—'It is the Spaniard that is to be feared: the Spaniard, who layeth his pretences and practices with a long hand.'

The way in which Ralegh tenders advice to his monarch

is very unlike the way in which he lectures his own
family. We could wish on the whole that Ralegh had not
written his *Instructions to his Son and to Posterity*. Here is a
Polonius indeed (but a really strong-minded Polonius,
whose advice is decidedly instruction) laying down the
law on friendship, marriage, conduct, servants, economy,
drink. The trouble with the instruction given is not that
it is always faulty or over-prudent, but that the motivat-
ing spirit is worldly, politic and calculating. The very
first chapter, on the choice of friends, is unpleasant in its
cunning and its eyeing of the main chance. Friendships
are never to be struck up with those who are poorer or
inferior in rank because those friends will pursue the
relationship for mercenary ends only, but 'let thy love
be to the best so long as they do well; but take heed that
thou love God, thy country, thy Prince and thine own
estate before all others.' Or again, 'Take also special
care that thou never trust any friend or servant with any
matter that may endanger thy estate.'

The almost fanatic concern for the preservation of one's
estate inspires all along the more repellent axioms. The
words about the settlement one ought to make for one's
wife are so remarkable that they should be given in full:

Let her have equal part of thy estate whilst thou livest, if
thou find her sparing and honest, but what thou givest after
thy death, remember that thou givest it to a stranger, and
most times to an enemy; for he that shall marry thy wife will
despise thee, thy memory and thine, and shall possess the
quiet of thy labours, the fruit which thou hast planted, enjoy
thy love and spend with joy and ease what thou hast spared
and gotten with joy and travail. Yet always remember that
thou leave not thy wife to be a shame unto thee after thou
art dead, but that she may live according to thy estate . . .
But howsoever it be, or whatsoever thou find, leave thy

wife no more than of necessity thou must, but only during her widowhood, for if she love again, let her not enjoy her second love in the same bed wherein she loved thee, nor fly to future pleasures with those feathers which Death hath pulled from thy wings, but leave thy estate to thy house and children in which thou livest upon earth whilst it lasteth.

The strange absence of any note of charity, love, liberality or selflessness is again impressive in a warning against borrowing and lending and standing surety. Take care, he says, 'that thou suffer not thyself to be wounded for other men's faults and scourged for other men's offences—which is, the surety for another, for thereby millions of men have been beggared and destroyed, paying the reckoning of other men's riot . . . If thou smart, smart for thine own sins, and, above all things, be not made an ass to carry the burdens of other men: if any friend desire thee to be his surety, give him a part of what thou hast to spare. If he press thee further, he is not thy friend at all.'

The end and aim of all the advice is self-interest. To see love of God conjoined with love of one's own estate, tempts us to think that the persuasion to godliness is but perfunctory and that Mammon is the real object of worship. And nowhere is there even lip-service paid to the other great commandment to love one's neighbour as oneself. But although the worldly wisdom of the homilies is suffocating, it is to be remembered that these injunctions are hardly intended by Ralegh to lay bare his 'philosophy of life'. Like some of Bacon's essays they have a limited end and narrow sphere of operation: they are specially designed as a guide to social behaviour in a particular social environment. In addition, it cannot be denied that a good deal of the advice is at least prudent and sensible and right-minded (though never great-hearted). The 'great care to be had in the choosing of a wife' has its moments as an essay in prose on the theme of 'conceit begotten by the eyes'. Even here, however, selfishness creeps in: he advises his son to take more care that his wife loves him 'rather than thyself besotted on her', but 'be not sour or stern to thy wife, for cruelty engendreth no other thing than hatred.'

It would be interesting to know how the *Instructions* were compiled; they often seem to bear the stamp of a man who has just been stung by a disappointment or a piece of treachery and in his immediate mortification makes a note in his commonplace book to warn others. 'If thou trust any servant with thy purse, be sure thou take his account before thou sleep.' It would also be interesting to know the date of composition, and whether the style was at all influenced by Bacon's *Essays*. 'Speaking much, also, is a sign of vanity; for he that is lavish in words is a niggard in deeds . . . He that cannot refrain from much speaking is like a city without walls and less pains in the world a man cannot take, than to hold his tongue.' But the style in general has the tone of the Hebrew prophet: some quotation from the chapter on 'what inconveniences happen to such as delight in wine' may serve to illustrate this and conclude the discussion of the work:

> A drunkard will never shake off the delight of beastliness, for the longer it possesseth a man, the more he will delight in it, and the older he groweth, the more he shall be subject to it, for it dulleth the spirits and destroyeth the body as ivy doth the old tree and as the worm that engendreth in the kernel of the nut.
>
> Take heed, therefore, that such a cureless canker pass not thy youth, nor such a beastly infection thy old age, for then shall all thy life be but as the life of a beast and, after

thy death, thou shalt only leave a shameful infamy to thy posterity, who shall study to forget that such a one was their father.

The difficulty with many of Ralegh's miscellaneous writings is that they hardly seem to be self-contained or completed works, or that they have perhaps been put together to serve some special purpose we know nothing about. *The Sceptic* is a translation from Sextus Empiricus, and we can only glean from other writings of Ralegh how far it is to be taken as representing his own views. The *Treatise on the Soul* one can hardly discuss at all without more knowledge. Strathmann, who calls it 'a summary of conventional beliefs', is not entirely certain of its authenticity; he suggests it may be rather an abstract of another work than an independent essay. It is certainly difficult to know what should have induced Ralegh to compose it, if he did. The modern reader who perseveres with the little treatise may feel the same impatience with the discussion that Ralegh himself felt with Ironside's attempts to define the nature of the soul.

No such lack of individuality marks a piece of a very different kind indeed, an essay on war, probably only in draft form or perhaps a fragment of a larger projected work, first printed in 1650 with the title *A Discourse of the Original and Fundamental Cause of Natural, Customary, Arbitrary, Voluntary and Necessary War*. This was probably written after *The History of the World*; Ralegh reflects on what must, after all his researches, have seemed the usual trade and occupation of mankind. Though ill-balanced as a whole, the essay is most powerfully written, and the attitude to war should be contrasted with that implied in the letter on the Cadiz action. It never enters Ralegh's head that war at any time is glorious; the farthest he goes in justifying it at all is to admit that it may be *necessary* to repel an invader and that it may be *legitimate* to occupy by force sparsely-inhabited regions—though he points out that there is no clear division between a harmless occupation and the abominable war of invasion which carries in its train the extermination of a native population. On the causes of war, Ralegh speaks often in terms a modern can understand—discontent and unemployment at home will often make a ruler find a pretext for a war, and so will a heavy increase of population and the consequent need for *lebensraum*. But the chief cause of the chief kind of war (arbitrary war) is, of course, ambition:

> To speak in general: whosoever hath dominion absolute over some one, authority less absolute over many more, will seek to draw those that are not wholly his own into entire subjection. It fares with politic bodies as with physical: each would convert all into their own proper substance, and cast forth as excrements what will not be changed.

Ralegh has the Elizabethan horror of civil war—'a greater plague cannot come upon a people'. Although he cannot share the Tudor belief in the divinity of monarchy, believing as he does that laws are man-made and can, theoretically, be changed by the will of man, he does argue that since human nature is imperfect, all human government is imperfect, and that it is far, far better to acquiesce in obedience to the established government than to institute chaos and anarchy by setting out to introduce another form of government by means of civil war. In any case, civil dissension never proceeds from principles or high motives: the perpetual restlessness of mankind is used by the avarice, ambition and vengefulness of the few. Liberty is but a word in the mouth in time of civil war: 'The common people of

L

England have suffered the same fate as other nations: they have been drawn with heat and fury to shed one another's blood for such a liberty as their leaders never intended they should have.' This thought leads Ralegh on to a great passage of pity for all who die in war ignorant of the base and selfish ends they have given their lives to promote:

> What deluded wretches, then, have a great part of mankind been, who have either yielded themselves to be slain in causes which, if truly known, their heart would abhor, or been the bloody executioners of other men's ambition! 'Tis a hard fate to be slain for what a man should never willingly fight, yet few soldiers have laid themselves down in the bed of honour under better circumstances.

Whether one agrees with Ralegh's attitude or not, the intellectual power of his work must be recognised; the insoluble puzzle is to know how the author could also be the author of *Instructions to his Son* and the compiler of *Maxims of State*.

We shall leave aside the multitude of short tracts which show the insatiable curiosity of Ralegh's mind, discourses on the invention of ships, on war with Spain, orders to be observed by commanders of his fleet, observations touching trade and commerce with the Hollander, and turn now to the great history of the world.

The Composition of The History of the World

Of his temerity in setting out, an ageing prisoner, to write a history of the world that should be no mere sketch or popular account, but a comprehensive record of all ages past, Ralegh was himself fully aware. 'In whom had there been no other defect (who am all defect) than the time of the day, it were enough: the day of a tempestuous life, drawn on to the very evening ere I began.' Had he started the work in his youth and freedom, 'I might yet well have doubted that the darkness of age and death would have covered over both it and me long before the performance'. An undertaking so preposterously difficult in the circumstances, none but a Ralegh would have had the daring to consider or the self-confidence to embark upon. It is Virginia and Guiana in the world of learning; not the diligence and the energy even of a Ralegh could carry the colossal project to completion. When the task was begun it is impossible to say: the plan must have been maturing in his mind for years, certainly before the 1607 (or 1608) often conjectured as a starting-point.[1] Some hint that the first volume was nearing its conclusion in 1611 is given by an entry in the Stationers' Register of that year, but it was not until 1614 that there appeared a folio without title-page, giving in 1,000,000 words the story of mankind from the Creation to Rome in the second century B.C. That Ralegh intended, and indeed had 'hewn out', a second and third volume, he tells us himself at the close of the first, adding that many discouragements 'persuaded his silence', including the death of the young Prince Henry, to whom the work had been directed. The work was well received by all save King James, who found his prisoner 'too saucy in censuring princes', and through the century it achieved a real eminence of favour, especially with the republicans: Cromwell recommended it, Milton used it. Ralegh's bibliographer, T. N. Brushfield,

---

[1] Ralegh's recently-found notebook (see pp. 48 and 101) gives us some conception of his preparations. We see him making an index of his geographical notes to help in his analysis of Old Testament history, carefully drawing his own maps, listing his books of reference. He apparently found more convenient methods of arranging his material, for this notebook was never filled. Since the poem at the end of the book probably belongs to the 1590's, it is possible that these preliminary workings were begun before the turn of the century.

gives a list of eleven editions published before the turn of the century. But fashions in history change: there seem to be only three editions between 1687 and the present day; the last edition was 1829. Matthew Arnold made a disparaging comparison of Ralegh's method with that of Thucydides. There are, however, some signs that the work is more charitably received than it was in the last century, though it must be confessed that no one would dream of turning to it as an authority. It is, frankly, not the history that really interests *us*; but that it is more than an empty monument of English prose, I shall try to demonstrate in the succeeding pages.

There has been some sharpness in the arguments on how much Ralegh was indebted to others in composing the *History*. It is not to be expected that such a work could have been written by the most learned historian (which Ralegh was not) without consultations with others any more than without using other men's books. Ben Jonson (in his cups) claimed that 'the best wits in England were employed for making of his History' and that he himself 'had written a piece to him of the Punic War which he [Ralegh] altered and set in his book'. What sounds in Jonson's mouth like the immoral employment of other men's brains is presumably only a rather extended use of any scholar's practice of asking for information and clarification among his acquaintances. For Ralegh, the physical difficulty of seeing all the works he wished to consult must have been great, and he must have been forced to rely upon learned friends more than he would have done had he had freedom of movement. Traditionally, among his helpers are named Dr. Robert Burhill (for 'Mosaic and Oriental antiquities'), Harriot and the two other 'magi' of Ralegh's fellow-prisoner Northumberland, and Sir John Hoskyns. Ralegh indi-

cates in the Preface the sort of consultation he practised,
when he acknowledges his ignorance of Hebrew and says
that occasionally he has 'borrowed the interpretation of
some of my learned friends.'

Rather more perturbing evidence of reliance on
others has been found in the first chapter, in the account
and explanation of the Creation. That much of Ralegh's
philosophy as revealed here is conventional and familiar
is immaterial: we have learned to expect from Ralegh the
rephrasing of traditional and time-honoured thought.
But it appears that the extremely learned citations of
authorities gathered at the foot of these early pages are
sometimes dust in the eyes of the reader. Dr. Arnold
Williams has explained[1] how anyone who wished to
gather all the opinions expressed by theologians on the
first three chapters of Genesis would find them most
conveniently collected for him in many commentaries.
Such a commentary was that of Benedict Pererius, *Com-
mentariorum et Disputionum in Genesin*. Ralegh hardly men-
tions Pererius in his footnotes, but Dr. Williams shows
that the impressive review of the schoolmen and church-
fathers is not based on original reading but is simply taken
out of Pererius's commentary, even to the point of fairly
close translation in the text itself. Once, indeed,
Ralegh slips in translation. 'Beroaldus affirmeth that
bdela in Hebrew signifieth "pearl": so doth Eugubinus; and
Jerome calls it "oleaster".' Unfortunately, in Pererius's
Latin text, Jerome Oleaster is the name of another
authority who supports the interpretation that *bdela*
means 'pearl'. This discovery of Ralegh's reliance on
ready-made commentaries does not mean that he has
surrendered his own interpretations and his liberty of

[1] *Studies in Philology*, xxxiv (1937), pp. 191–208. Pererius's commentary
is in the list of his books in Ralegh's notebook.

conjecture. But before we congratulate Ralegh on the wide reading he undertook for his *History*, we must remember such short cuts as these which he ingeniously and silently took.

The Purpose of History

In composing a history of the world, Ralegh gives very much more than a record of events. To begin with, 'history' is an all-embracing term: almost every known branch of learning is used or discussed in the work—philosophy, theology, comparative religion, ethics, geography, astronomy and astrology, political theory, biblical criticism, and the art of war. This is so, not because, as an historian, Ralegh likes to indulge in asides or in a little trespass outside his province, or even that his work must take cognisance of the fruits of research in other branches of knowledge. There is simply no segmentation of these different learnings; Ralegh's study is Man, and all aspects of that study are as one. An account of Man which concentrated on political history or social history would have seemed false and partial history. Ralegh begins his *History* at the Creation not merely because he must begin at the beginning, but because he cannot separate history from metaphysics, and the history of man is meaningless unless prefaced with a conception of the nature of man, his relation with God and the purpose of his being on earth at all. Like the ideal epic poem, Ralegh's *History* was to expound 'all ye know and all ye need to know'; it is indeed an interpretation of man, explained in terms of his history.

Again, the notion of history as a faithful presentation of the events of the past for the reader to find what interpretation and derive what profit he can from them was quite foreign to Renaissance ideas. No historian considered an accumulation of accurate facts as his objective. The 'ending end of all earthly learning', said Sir Philip Sidney, is 'virtuous action'. Knowledge for knowledge sake was meaningless; knowledge was for the betterment of the individual and society, and the scholar had to make clear the present and immediate value of his researches. History was understood to be a study of the past undertaken in order to throw light on the events of the present—and what had no contemporary application was not worth the recording. From a study of history, Puttenham the rhetorician said, a man learns 'what is the best course to be taken in all his actions and advices in this world'. Ralegh is at one with his age in considering history to be justified only in so far as it serves to instruct men how to behave in the sight of their fellow-men and in the sight of God. His great Preface is called by a modern scholar the 'fullest and most inspired expression' of 'the great tradition' of the Renaissance view of the use of history.[1]

History, Ralegh explains, multiplies almost infinitely the experience available to any one man in his lifetime; history 'hath given us life in our understanding', we behold plainly our long dead ancestors living again and by the example of their fortunes and follies learn what, in our own lives or our own society, is meet to be followed and pursued. 'We may gather out of history a policy no less wise than eternal, by the comparison and application of other men's fore-passed miseries with our own like errors and ill-deservings.' In the body of the *History* we find scattered such observations as that the 'end and scope of all history [is] to teach by examples of time past such wisdom as may guide our desires and actions' (II, 21, vi).

[1] L. B. Campbell, *Shakespeare's 'Histories'* (1947), p. 80.

The doctrine that history must always convey its lesson to modern times can be seen on the pragmatic level in the realm of social conduct and of state 'policy'. Ralegh always draws the moral of the story. Darius fights the invader Alexander instead of breaking his fury by delaying tactics (IV, 2, iii). 'The invaded', comments Ralegh, 'ought evermore to fight upon the advantage of time and place. Because we read histories to inform our understanding by the examples therein found, we will give some instances of those that have perished by adventuring in their own countries to charge an invading army . . .' Asides like this are everywhere to be seen. Opening the *History* quite at random, one finds that the life of the king Amazia gives rise to a very interesting little essay on the uselessness of a regime of severity to cover weakness in the personality of the ruler. A section on the strife of the Carthaginians with their mercenaries is followed by a long section of general reflection on a tyranny and its consequences. Every effect noted in the *History* is given a cause—'Such was the recompense of his treachery . . .' Every incident is searched for its bearing on matters of general interest. What Ralegh gathers from the story of Samson is amusing enough (II, 15, i). The first comment is on Samson's mother being forbidden strong drink during her pregnancy: 'it seemeth that many women of this age have not read, or at least will not believe this precept; the most part forbearing not drinks; . . . filling themselves with all sorts of wines and with artificial drinks far more forcible: by reason whereof, so many wretched feeble bodies are born into the world, and the races of the able and strong men in effect decayed.'

But although this kind of moralising, in things both of little and great importance in worldly action, is rooted in Ralegh's method, and although it gives a constant alertness to all he says, for not an action is noted unless it can be made to bear fruit, yet it is but dallying beside the main purpose of the *History*. Ralegh's phrase was 'a policy no less wise than eternal' and that which really inspires him is not worldly wisdom but the desire to show how human history, which is a record of God's providence and His judgments on the deeds of mankind, provides constant lessons to all who study it, princes and private men, how to frame their lives in a manner acceptable to God. For Ralegh, God is with mankind from the beginning to the end of Time, punishing and rewarding and bringing to pass in every least action. So that in writing history, we teach by the examples of the rise and fall of great men and great nations 'for what virtue and piety God made prosperous and for what vice and deformity he made wretched'. 'God's judgments upon the greater and the greatest have been left to posterity, first, by those happy hands which the Holy Ghost hath guided [in the Old Testament], and secondly by their virtue who have gathered the acts and ends of men mighty and remarkable in the world [historians].' Since God's judgments do not vary, what his providence and justice allotted to past ages and different empires he will allot to our own day and age. 'We find that God is everywhere the same God.'

> The judgments of God are for ever unchangeable; neither is he wearied by the long process of time and won to give his blessing in one age to that which he hath cursed in another. Wherefore those that are wise, or whose wisdom, if it be not great, yet is true and well grounded, will be able to discern the bitter fruits of irreligious policy, as well among those examples that are found in ages removed far from the present as in those of latter times.

To prove how the examples of past times act as a warning to men of the present to avoid incurring the wrath of God, Ralegh in his Preface runs rapidly—and devastatingly—through the lives of the kings of England pointing out their viciousness and the harvest they reaped.

Such then is the purpose and intention Ralegh had in compiling a history of the world. Not to present only an accurate record of the main events of the past, but to give a picture of man, his nature and development, for the purpose of inculcating in his readers the wisdom they needed so to guide their steps in this world as to achieve God's blessing. This aim Ralegh shares with all his contemporaries who dealt with the past, whether it be Shakespeare in his historical plays or Holinshed in his Chronicles.

Ralegh's Philosophy of History

The philosophy of history implied by the purpose Ralegh entertains is primarily that of the Old Testament. Nothing comes to pass that God does not bring about, and all suffering and affliction are to be explained as God's punishment for iniquity, whether in states or individuals. Ralegh naturally has to emphasize that God's intervention does not work directly, but through material agents; conversely he must emphasize that all material events are purposeful and illustrate God's way of directing human fortunes. A tyranny is as much a visitation to a state as sickness is to an individual; 'It pleaseth God sometimes to punish his people by a tyrannous hand.' Suffering is from a just God: 'the impiety of man is the forcible attractive of God's vengeance.' Ralegh blames men for imputing 'famine, plagues, war, loss, vexation, death, sickness and calamities' only to natural and human causes 'which as being next their eyes and ears seem to them to

work every alteration that happeneth'. God's reasons
may be mysterious to man, but these things must be
explained as punishment for sin.[1] Naturally, the reconciliation of what ordinarily seem to mortal men to be the
causes of things with the notion that God brings all about
needs much explanation. In an important section
(II, 21, vi), Ralegh discusses frankly the difficulties which
an historian with his philosophy of history has in account-
ing for the motives of men. The Old Testament prophets
refer all to the will of God and (for a judicious historian)
are rather awkwardly silent about the direct and immediate human motives for actions. The historian is little
better off with profane history; 'the heart of man is
unsearchable'; a motive is given in terms of personality,
perhaps, but if we could go deeper we should find more
convincing and compelling reasons why a man acted as he
did. Darius fought the Greeks to extend his Empire,
but also because his wife wanted Greek women for
slaves. The historian must do the best he can: he must
look deeply for the most likely human motives and
realize that his best knowledge will be only conjecture, and he must refer all things finally to the will of
God.

History is not just a repetition of God's blows upon
mankind. An inscrutable plan is being unfolded and the
great figures of the past, good and bad, are the agents of
this plan. Ralegh reflects on Alexander the Great:

For so much hath the spirit of some one man excelled, as it
hath undertaken and effected the alteration of the greatest
states and commonweals, the erection of monarchies, the

[1] There is no doubt that Ralegh's view of history takes colour from the
sources he is using, and the long passages of Hebrew history are very much
more determinedly presented in terms of God's providence than passages
where he followed, not the Old Testament, but, say, Thucydides. But the
difference is only one of degree.

conquest of kingdoms and empires; guided handfuls of men against multitudes of equal bodily strength, contrived victories beyond all hope and discourse of reason . . .; such spirits have been stirred up in sundry ages of the world, and in divers parts thereof, to erect and cast down again, to establish and to destroy, and to bring all things, persons and states to the same certain ends which the infinite spirit of the Universal, piercing, moving and governing all things, hath ordained.

It follows that there can be no greater arrogance than for man to congratulate himself on the victories that fall to his hand—'everyone striving to magnify himself whilst all forget God'.

Whatever evidence he may find of God's plan in the evolution of history, Ralegh is bemused by no theory of progress and improvement as he watches the development of civilization. There is change indeed, but not towards an earthly paradise, for man rejects God the more and is therefore punished the more as he grows more civilized. Ralegh shared with his age, the age that was rapidly passing, the belief that man's days, which could be counted from their beginning, were not fulfilling anything in themselves and that Time must shortly have a stop, 'the long day of mankind drawing fast towards an evening and the world's tragedy and time near at an end'. None the less, the problem of the evolution of culture interested him, even though he did not take the standpoint of the enthusiastic Baconian watching the growing light of knowledge and power. His learning was sufficient to find in many non-communicating cultures the same legends, the same stages in the use of tools and the discovering of arts, crafts and letters, the same patterns of development in morals, religion and customs, in ways of dwelling and building, and in forms of government. He therefore conceives of a natural law of development:

> As the same infinite God is present with all his creatures, so hath he given the same invention to divers nations, whereof the one hath not had commerce with the other.

Civilization develops in complexity, but man does not develop in goodness and wisdom. Man multiplies his viciousness as he increases his power over nature, and all that he builds will pass away. 'Time will also take revenge of the excess which it hath brought forth.'

Such then, very briefly sketched, is Ralegh's general philosophy of history, which enables him to entertain his belief in the use of history. We shall have to return to his philosophy, in order to show how, within the larger concept of God's providence, Ralegh views and judges the actions of men. Meanwhile, we have to examine the way Ralegh tackles the many thorny problems confronting him in trying to set out the story of humanity.

Chronology and Miracles

The modern reader will find the contents-list of *The History of the World* exceedingly odd. The problems of chronology presented by Genesis and the Old Testament have ceased to worry us; the life-spans of the patriarchs, the location of Paradise, the kind of wood used for the Ark, are no longer of vital concern to the serious historian. The space given to the retelling of Hebrew history would seem less disproportionate had Ralegh carried his work on to later volumes, but even so, the attention he gives it shows that the various epochs had a quite different value for Ralegh than for us and that he had a loyalty to the Old Testament as an historical record

which a later age has rejected. Fidelity to the Bible is
the cause of most of the strangeness of the appearance
of the *History* and also the cause of most of Ralegh's difficulties in arranging his account of human affairs.

In the first place, there is 'that never resolved question and labyrinth of times'. Within the Old Testament
there was a host of difficulties in establishing the proper
dating of the events described, and then there was the
problem of dovetailing into it the pagan records of antiquity. The difficulties of chronology that faced the
Renaissance historian and the solutions which Ralegh
put forward have been fully analysed by E. R. Strathmann:
the enormous concern Ralegh had about the problems is
evident in almost every chapter of the *History* and in the
formidable chronological table in which Ralegh sets out
his synchronisation of the various records available to him.
Professor Strathmann has high praise for Ralegh's 'stu-
dious industry', and if we may tend to regret that so much
diligence and time had to be spent in attempting to
reconcile the irreconcilable, we can at least admire the
seriousness and sobriety of Ralegh's methods. Cardinal
with Ralegh is the truth of the Bible: to reconcile the
Bible with itself he is prepared to spend all the endeavours of reason. Where in the end it is not possible to
square differences and disagreements, as in the question
of the length of time between the Flood and the birth
of Abraham, it is not the Bible, but man's imperfect
understanding that is to be blamed. Ralegh has not
reached his confidence in the inviolability of the Scriptures without great struggle; like Sir Thomas Browne,
he has fought the battle of Lepanto within himself. But
having determined that, in spite of apparent inconsisten-
cies and absurdities, the Bible presents an accurate record
of history, he is prepared to go to infinite pains to

explain as reasonable what may seem dark to human understanding. Chapter Seven of the first book, an account of the Flood, is one of profound interest as an example of Ralegh's method. He takes in every account of the great floods of antiquity, assesses with scrupulous care the evidence on the various problems associated with the story—his witnesses ranging from Galileo to soothsayers he has spoken with in America. The whole exposition is a remarkable example of Ralegh's 'use of new learning to bolster old belief', to use Professor Strathmann's phrase.

The details of Ralegh's chronological struggles need not concern us: his acceptance, for example, of Egyptian records but his denial that they can be taken at their face value as appearing to prove 'men before Adam'. But there are other difficulties the solving of which provides a good deal that is of interest to the modern reader, like the relation of ancient non-biblical legends and early history to the Old Testament. His attitude to pagan legends in general is that they are dark expressions of truths to be found in the Scriptures:

> Now as Cain was the first Jupiter, and from whom also the Ethnicks had the invention of sacrifice: so were Jubal, Tubal and Tubalcain (inventors of pastorage, smithscraft and music) the same which were called by the ancient profane writers Mercurius, Vulcan and Apollo . . .

Although the muddle is sometimes appalling, when Moses, Prometheus, Hercules, Hermes Trismegistus and Aesculapius are all thrown together and their achievements rationally discussed, one has to admire Ralegh for his earnestness within the framework of his assumptions. And his conviction, in dealing with Greek legends, that 'most fables and poetical fictions were occasioned by some ancient truth, which either by ambiguity of speech or some allusion they did maimedly and darkly express' anticipates modern reconstructions of the historicity of the legendary heroes of Greece and Crete—even though his own rationalising of Minos or Oedipus may not provide food for more than amusement.[1]

As with chronology and pre-history, so with miracles: the testimony of Scripture must not be impeached, but must be supported by every effort of reason. This is not to say that Ralegh tries to explain away miracles by a naturalistic interpretation—quite the reverse. The passage of the Israelites across the Red Sea (II, 3, viii) is discussed with an awe-inspiring fund of information, geographical and scientific, to prove that the rolling back of the waters could have come about in no other way but by the direct hand of God.

But in spite of our admiration for the intellectual energy Ralegh shows, it is undoubtedly a relief to turn from his attempts to use the Old Testament as a basis for the early history of mankind and make it yield a reasonable account (wrestlings which Ralegh's faith demanded and which ours does not) to the less debatable ground of Greek and Roman history. There the settling of problems which by their nature cannot be settled, no longer hinders the unrolling of Ralegh's map of human achievement.

The Death of Ambition

The shortest way to describe Ralegh's attitude to those achievements of man which it is his task to record is to say that he thinks precious little of them. There was

[1] Ralegh's method should not be confused with that of Bacon, who, in his *Wisdom of the Ancients* (published about the same time as this part of the *History* may have been written), interpreted Greek legends as allegories of fundamental human experience.

surely never an historian who looked at his subject with eyes so disillusioned as Ralegh's. He is quite impervious to the romance and glory of high endeavour in war and empire. By greatness he remains totally unmoved. Human history is for him a sorry record of ambition, greed, lust, selfishness and blindness. Not Athens nor Rome nor England inspires him to lyrical enthusiasm. Alexander the Great is one of those 'troublers of the world who have bought their glory with so great destruction and effusion of blood'. His valour and courage Ralegh admits, but valour is a quality 'taken by itself, not much to be admired': 'If adventurous natures were to be commended simply, we should confound that virtue with the hardiness of thieves, ruffians, and mastiff dogs.' Valour is 'no way praiseworthy but in daring good things'.

Nationalism was a very common element in Renaissance historiography; indeed, the praise of one's native country was often a leading consideration of the historian. Ralegh is remarkably immune from local prejudices. He is even able to give whole-hearted praise to the dauntlessness of the Spaniards in opening up the New World. Certainly, in a famous passage, he preferred English soldiers to those of other countries and ages, but as he also considered that nothing moved soldiers to brave deeds except lust for spoils, that perhaps is no high praise. His swift and scathing review of the record of English kings in the Preface has already been mentioned, 'who, having beheld, both in divine and human letters, the success of infidelity, injustice and cruelty, have notwithstanding planted after the same pattern'. There is an eloquent silence on the reign of Elizabeth, but it is not merely Richard II and Richard III, but Henry VII and Henry VIII, who seem to Ralegh not builders of the

M

nation's greatness, but patterns of mercilessness and
'policy'.

Those whom the world honours are honoured for
unworthy qualities. Flatterers, for example, 'are a kind
of vermin which poison all the princes of the world, and
yet they prosper better than the worthiest and valiantest
men do ; and I wonder not at it, for it is a world, and as our
Saviour Christ hath told us, *The World will love her own*.'
The discussion of Fortune in the first chapter of the work
specifically equates great place and earthly prosperity with
denial of virtue. Anyone who wishes to succeed in
society or empire must advance himself by hypocrisy,
time-serving and unscrupulousness and must forswear
honesty, truth and probity. Too few, holds Ralegh,
understand this distinction between real virtue and what
the world calls virtue; the most acclaim and applaud as
greatness that which is really vice.

History, then, is a record of the actions of kings inspired by ambition and lust for fame and power. They
think only of the meretricious world and ignore the
interminable lessons of the instability and insufficiency
of its rewards; they discover too late the teachings of
Time and Death, which rob all victories of their sweetness. Ambition, the prime mover of the famous, is the
primal sin, the cardinal denial of truth: it is a monster
that in its destructiveness and sterility denies and rages
against the harmony of things, against nature. All other
passions are sometimes cooled. 'But ambition which
begetteth every vice and is itself the child and darling of
Satan looketh only towards ends by itself set down, forgetting nothing (how fearful and inhuman soever) which
may serve it; remembering nothing, whatsoever justice,
piety, right or religion can offer and allege on the contrary.' To be ambitious is to try to make oneself like the

Almighty, which is 'damnable pride'; princes should rather seek 'the blessedness promised by our Saviour unto the peacemakers'. That fine discourse on tyranny already referred to (V, 2, ii, sub-section 4), ends with a comment on the extreme rarity of the really Christian king, whose actions are inspired by a love of the general good, perfected by its reference to 'the fountain of all goodness'. 'Of christian kings, if there were many such, the world would soon be happy.'

It is paradoxical that a History undertaken to warn man to avoid conduct leading to damnation and disaster should at the same time be a sombre dissertation on the unteachability of man. Inevitably, Ralegh says, men seek the pleasures and gifts of this world and take no account of the misery they bring to themselves and to others in encompassing them. Ralegh's *History* exhibits danger-signals to a mankind he knows will not heed them. Having completed, in the Preface, his minatory pageant of godless kings he shrugs his shoulders:

> But what of all this? And to what end do we lay before the eyes of the living the fall and fortunes of the dead, seeing the world is the same that it hath been, and the children of the present time will still obey their parents?

No sooner has he expressed his faith in the value of history as an instruction in godliness (see above, p. 151), than he continues with a gesture of despair:

> But it is neither of examples the most lively instruction nor the words of the wisest men, nor the terror of future torments, that hath yet so wrought in our blind and stupefied minds as to make us remember that the infinite eye and wisdom of God doth pierce through all our pretences; as to make us remember that the justice of God doth require none other accuser than our own consciences; which neither

the false beauty of our apparent actions, nor all the form-
ality which (to pacify the opinions of men) we put on, can
in any or the least kind, cover from his knowledge.

Ralegh balances an absolute contempt of what the
world has to offer with an absolute conviction that the
world will inveigle man into serving it. The Preface
hammers home in its magnificent prose the doctrine that
the attaining of material objectives has nothing to do with
that quietness of conscience in the hope of eternal life
which alone sanctifies existence. Honour and dynastic
security are equally false gods. Whatever in this world
we are mad enough to set store by, to struggle and strive
after, age withers and death destroys, and it is only with
the approach of death that we realise the futility of our
endeavours and the godlessness of our lives. 'It is then
that we cry out to God for mercy; then, when ourselves
can no longer exercise cruelty to others, and it is only
then that we are strucken through the soul with this
terrible sentence, *that God will not be mocked*.' In a passage of great dignity, he sets out the inevitable failure of
all that which, being offered by the world, is therefore
subject to Time and Death:

> For be it that we have lived many years and (according to
> Solomon) *in them all we have rejoiced*, or be it that we have
> measured the same length of days and therein have evermore
> sorrowed; yet looking back from our present being, we find
> both the one and the other, to wit, the joy and the woe,
> sailed out of sight; and Death, which doth pursue us and hold
> us in chase from our infancy, hath gathered it . . . So as
> whosoever he be, to whom Fortune hath been a servant and
> the time a friend, let him but take the accompt of his
> memory (for we have no other keeper of our pleasures past)
> and truly examine what it hath reserved either of beauty
> and youth or foregone delights; what it hath saved, that it

might last, of his dearest affections or of whatever else the amorous springtime gave his thoughts of contentment, then unvaluable; and he shall find that all the art which his elder years have can draw no other vapour out of these dissolutions than heavy, secret and sad sighs. He shall find nothing remaining but those sorrows which grow up after our fast-springing youth, overtake it when it is at a stand, and overtop it utterly when it begins to wither; insomuch as looking back from the very instant time and from our now-being, the poor, diseased and captive creature hath as little sense of all his former miseries and pains as he that is most blessed in common opinion hath of his forepassed pleasures and delights. For whatsoever is cast behind us is just nothing, and what is to come, deceitful hope hath it . . . Only those few black swans I must except: who, having had the grace to value worldly vanities at no more than their own price, do, by retaining the comfortable memory of a well-acted life, behold death without dread and the grave without fear, and embrace both as necessary guides to endless glory.

So does Ralegh write his 'Even such is time' in prose, and so does he generalize, as he sets out on his history of the world, on the particular activities of the great ones of the earth he is about to set before the reader. The *History* is bounded by this statement in the Preface, and the famous invocation to death which concludes the work.

How death robs the victor of his conquests and time defaces the monuments of the Emperor, is, then, the constant theme of the work. It is hard to refrain from very liberal quotation, so brilliantly does the theme of *tempus edax rerum* inspire Ralegh to write. One very short passage has both a literal and a symbolic value: idolatry and its monuments pass away from the earth, but modern man also worships idols—'the high and shining idol of glory, the all-commanding image of bright gold'—and these profanities too will pass away as though they had never been:

> Jupiter is no more vexed with Juno's jealousies: Death hath persuaded him to chastity and her to patience; and that Time which hath devoured itself hath also eaten up both the bodies and images of him and his: yea, their stately temples of stone and dureful marble . . . There are now none in Phoenicia that lament the death of Adonis, nor any in Libya, Creta, Thessalia or elsewhere that can ask counsel or help from Jupiter. The great god Pan hath broken his pipes . . .

Civilization is ostentation and vanity: war is horror and cruelty; conquest is ambition; honour is bought with damnation: and Time and Death erase them all. *The History of the World* moves solemnly and inevitably to the concluding chapter:

> By this which we have already set down, is seen the beginning and end of the three first monarchies of the world, whereof the founders and erectors thought that they could never have ended. That of Rome which made the fourth was also at this time almost at the highest. We have left it flourishing in the middle of the field . . . but after some continuance it shall begin to lose the beauty it had; the storms of ambition shall beat her great boughs and branches one against another; her leaves shall fall off, her limbs wither, and a rabble of barbarous nations enter the field and cut her down.

We complain, seeing this transitoriness, of the instability of Fortune; we do not understand that all worldly empire is bound to be ephemeral; we go on, lusting after fame and continuing to build up by cruelty and oppression new walls over the old ruins, until death teaches us, too, how futile are our endeavours. 'Death, which hateth and destroyeth man, is believed; God, which hath made him and loves him, is always deferred.'

> O eloquent, just and mighty death! whom none could advise, thou hast persuaded; what none hath dared, thou hast done; and whom all the world hath flattered, thou only hast cast out of the world and despised; thou hast drawn together all the far-stretched greatness, all the pride, cruelty and ambition of man, and covered it all over with these two narrow words, *Hic jacet*.

The Style of the 'History'

The greatest writing in the *History* is in the passages of general reflection we have been quoting from. Even though the quotations are not so full as they should be to give the proper flavour of Ralegh's prose, their length will indicate how Ralegh achieves his effects not by the single pregnant or illuminating phrase, but by the onward surge of a paragraph. His prose is like the sea whose majesty is not in single waves but in the piling up of wave upon wave against the shore. Long and intricate sentences and balanced clauses build up passage after passage of solemnity and dignity. The rhythm is never staccato, but is sometimes kept moving and flowing almost for a whole folio page before it sinks to rest. One example will serve to show the architecture of his prose; in the following passage he is talking of the seven ages of man and has come to describe the last, which is compared to Saturn:

> wherein our days are sad and overcast, and in which we find by dear and lamentable experience and by the loss which can never be repaired, that of all our vain passions and affections past, the sorrow only abideth. Our attendants are sicknesses and variable infirmities, and by how much the more we are accompanied with plenty, by so much the more greedily is our end desired, whom when Time hath made

unsociable to others, we become a burthen to ourselves, being of no other use than to hold the riches we have from our successors. In this time it is, when (as aforesaid) we for the most part, and never before, prepare for our eternal habitation, which we pass on unto with many sighs, groans and sad thoughts, and in the end by the workmanship of death finish the sorrowful business of a wretched life, towards which we always travel both sleeping and waking: neither have those beloved companions of honour and riches any power at all to hold us any one day, by the glorious promise of entertainments; but by what crooked path soever we walk, the same leadeth on directly to the house of death, whose doors lie open at all hours and to all persons. For this tide of man's life, after it once turneth and declineth, ever runneth with a perpetual ebb and falling stream, but never floweth again; our leaf once fallen, springeth no more, neither doth the sun or the summer adorn us again with the garments of new leaves and flowers.   (I, 2, v).

Though the imagery is often formal and conventional and too little varied, metaphorical writing often brings great power. When he talks of the blindness of the Greeks to their danger from Philip, he writes: 'Indeed it was not in their philosophy to consider that all great alterations are stormlike, sudden and violent, and that then it is overlate to repair the decayed and broken banks when great rivers are once swollen, fast-running and enraged.'

It must be said that Ralegh's narrative style, though never dull, is not the most brilliant. Not that there is not vividness: the story of Alexander moves in alert fashion, enlivened by sudden sallies of the historic present. Indeed, the chapter on Alexander is probably the very best in the work; for narrative, description, reflection and interpretation, it is a typical example of Ralegh's methods and an outstanding example of his style. He seems to have absorbed and assimilated his material and to be writing from himself. Elsewhere, Ralegh seems unable to make the actions of the past live with the vividness he had given in his younger years to the accounts of actions in which he had himself taken part. But it is a saving grace of the *History* that both matter and manner are made fresh and insistent by the constant introduction of contemporary events. These intercalations show how alive Ralegh's own imagination was and how much history was for him what he claimed it to be—a comment from the past on the sort of actions and experiences undergone by modern man. There can be nothing dead in history to a man for whom every least incident stirs his memory and brings out a parallel incident from his own experience. And the reader's imagination also is kept alert by being constantly reminded of the unfailing relevance of history. Ralegh never fails to write interestingly when he dips into the rich store-house of his experience, and the style of the *History* is kept abundantly alive by his asides. He relates the smoking out of the enemy from the caves of Languedoc during the French civil wars, his landing at Fayal, the assault on Cadiz. Sometimes it is just an anecdote: Alexander's intolerance of an insult recalls Sir John Perrot's famous scoff at Elizabeth, which more than anything else caused his ruin; the furnishing of the dark corridors of history by conjecture he compares to the inventiveness of mapmakers, and relates the story of Don Pedro de Sarmiento, Ralegh's prisoner, who put an island in a map to please his wife. Towards the end of the work, when Ralegh has presumably realized that he will never extend his history to modern times, there is a far greater introduction of parallels and illustrations, not only from Ralegh's experience, but from the whole of modern history. It is very important to remember that the dipping into his own memory and the drawing of parallels ancient and modern are not tokens of a meandering, conversational attitude to history, but evidence of the way in which Ralegh's whole mind was engaged on what he was writing. Nothing was foreign, nothing separate and useless. Like the poet that he was, his whole experience, in seemingly distinct spheres, stood alert and at call to furnish an illustration or provide a comment.

Video meliora proboque; *deteriora sequor*. One would think, as Ralegh drives home the shining moral of his *History*, that all the lusting after the rewards of men and the battling for might and empire are but the building of Babel, impious strivings that cannot buy lasting satisfaction in this life and forbid all hope of salvation—one would think that he had achieved in himself that patience and wisdom and understanding, that clear-eyed rejection of the world with its storms and strains and false values, which came to King Lear as he went prisonwards:

> so we'll live
> And pray, and sing, and tell old tales, and laugh
> At gilded butterflies and hear (poor rogues)
> Talk of court-news, and we'll talk with them too—
> Who loses and who wins, who's in, who's out,
> And take upon's the mystery of things
> As if we were God's spies. And we'll wear out,
> In a wall'd prison, packs and sects of great ones,
> That ebb and flow by the moon.

Upon such sacrifices the gods indeed throw incense. But Ralegh was still to give the most frightening confirmation of his own vision of unteachable man, who will not, because he cannot, renounce his affection for what the world has to offer. Two years after the publication of the *History of the World* Ralegh wins his freedom to prosecute his mad endeavour in Guiana, to win back those things his words had constantly and insistently declared to be a nothingness: honour, position and wealth. He denied his own better knowledge in coveting those things, and the utter and wretched failure of his mission is really the final word and seal upon his historian's survey of the futility of ambition.

When is it that we examine this great account? Never while we have one vanity left us to spend; we plead for titles till our breath fail us, dig for riches whiles our strength enableth us, exercise malice while we can revenge, and then, when Time hath beaten from us both youth, pleasure and health, and that nature itself hateth the house of old age, we remember with Job that we must go the way from whence we shall not return, and that our bed is made ready for us in the dark . . .

But what examples have ever moved us? What persuasions reformed us? Or what threatenings made us afraid? We behold other men's tragedies played before us; we hear what is promised and threatened; but the world's bright glory hath put out the eyes of our minds, and these betraying lights (with which we only see) do neither look up towards termless joys nor down towards endless sorrows, till we neither know nor can look for anything else at the world's hands.

Chapter Five

CONCLUSION

I WANT now to ask what kind of epitaph Ralegh's most remarkable and versatile career deserves. Of course, its very complexity forbids a single coherent verdict. Do we think of him as the superb favourite of Elizabeth or the broken victim of James? Do we think of him as he plans the colonization of the New World or as he writes, in prison, an outstanding poem and an outstanding history? Do we think of him as he faces his accusers at Westminster Hall or as he inscribes his worldly-wise instructions to his son? It is not easy to sum up a man so various.

Ralegh's public career is in itself an extraordinary story. The moral judgment is that which has most perplexed historians. But it ought not to be difficult to see that Ralegh was neither a saint nor a megalomaniac: that he was capable of being magnanimous, splendid and honourable as well as petty, ruthless and hypocritical. The great Elizabethans will often contain within themselves such moral contradictions; to be aware of the coexistence of extremes is the important point. I have no desire at all to present Ralegh as a man without a darker side to his character. Ben Jonson said of him that he 'esteemed more of fame than conscience'. 'Fame' is the wrong word. Ralegh was ambitious, but it was something more than desire for place and wealth that drove him to undertake those enterprises which awe us by their number and vastness. Whatever it was that possessed him, it is certain that to attain the end was more important than not to outstep the bounds of friendship, decency and justice. 'I know he can toil terribly,' said Cecil. By sheer force of personality, he raised himself and set forward his projects at court, at sea, in administration. His career was that of a fast-moving stream which is impatient of obstacles and everlastingly changes course: having no other object than to reach the sea. His restless determination made him at times behave in an immoral way. Even so, let us admit that to weigh the number of his moral against his immoral actions helps us very little with Ralegh; what is more profitable is to perceive something of the quality of his imagination, and that, of course, involves things besides action and politics.

Ralegh's achievements as a poet do not bring him into the company of the greatest, nor would they, I think, even were a great deal more of his poetry discovered. But without inviting comparison with Shakespeare and Donne, or Spenser and Marlowe, I put him very high among the poets of his day. He is an under-estimated poet: partly because so much of the verse has been lost for so long, the remains even now being scrappy, and partly because it is so easy to be defeated by *Cynthia* that too few readers have given it a chance to gain their real affection. Ralegh has a gift of compelling speech, which makes new and urgent the comparatively ordinary. In talking of the verse I stressed that it was obedient to the conventions and practices of the time. But then, so was Shakespeare's. Ralegh can write with a kind of directness which makes him strongly independent of his age. He has written one or two perfect lyrics, and if his major poem were a little less fitful in its flame he would receive more of the acknowledgement which he deserves.

His prose writing has suffered less in reputation than his verse. Although *The History of the World* has been forgotten, its Preface has always been known and admired, along with the action-narrative of the *Revenge*. His prose, although its variety is one of its most impressive qualities, cannot show Nashe's exuberance, Hooker's grace or the terseness of Bacon's *Essays*, but for prose that *surges*, sweeping the reader on for sentence after sentence on a succession of subtly varying cadences, I would not look elsewhere than to Ralegh's meditations on Time and Ambition.

What is most striking about Ralegh's verse and prose is that they should be written by a man whose active career alone would use up more than the whole lifetime of most other people. The indomitable energy is not alone the marvel, but that one man should choose and be able to fulfil himself in so many different spheres. Not in any one kind of activity did he find his real satisfaction, whether it was writing a poem, composing a history or planning an expedition, but in all together. The full expression of his imagination was his whole life. He was fortunate to live in an age when art and life were as closely wedded as they have ever been. Literature and learning and action were all essential parts of his being. He was as much the dedicated artist as Milton or James Joyce, but his art had a medium wider than words and ideas. His epic was himself, with his poetry and his personal ambition, his explorations into science and into goldfields, his fighting and his meditation.

But it is truer to say that what Ralegh writes on these pages containing Guiana, Cadiz, *The Ocean to Cynthia*, *The History of the World*, the Tower and the scaffold, is not an epic but a tragedy. Ralegh had an imagination which saw goals undreamed of by lesser men and he shrank from no toil to achieve them. The vision which Christopher Marlowe turned into drama, Ralegh tried to translate into life. But to turn vision into reality would have needed means far beyond the compass of the greatest man. None of Ralegh's great schemes came to successful fruition. Virginia uncolonised, Guiana unexploited, the *History* uncompleted, he ends his life on the scaffold with his estate in ruins. The fragments of these unfinished or unsuccessful enterprises are awe-inspiring, but they are fragments. His real successes are very few. It is not far from the truth to say that he left behind him no mark except in men's memories and in the work of those who carried on his efforts in America.

I do not suggest that Ralegh's tragedy is of the Faustian kind: that he sold his soul to obtain more than humanity is allowed and ended in despair. There are tragedies of subtler quality than this. He aimed too high and failed, but the end he came to was not a simple result of aiming too high: his story is not one of sin and retribution, or, on the other hand, of totally undeserved suffering. Of his last expedition, Ralegh wrote: 'True it is that as many things succeeded both against reason and against our best endeavours, so it is most true that men are the causes of their own miseries, as I was of mine . . .' What a man hopes for and takes steps to bring about is one thing, what actually results is quite another. 'Our thoughts are ours, their ends none of our own.' Yet the end which comes about, and is so unlooked for, still bears indelibly the stamp of the man who planned and desired. Men who end as Ralegh ended have their own responsibility for their fate, but they share that responsibility with a whole army of forces beyond their control.

Errors and flaws in the man's character and judgment combine with other elements to bring him down. The malevolence of others helped to defeat Ralegh, though he in some measure wilfully incurred that malevolence. Plans which were good plans came to nothing because the time was not ripe for them, nor the materials to complete them yet available. Though it is dangerous to talk about the spirit of the age as a positive force, yet it is true that a current which carried Ralegh along to prosperity and success under Elizabeth changed its direction under James and abandoned him in shallows. In all there was the inevitability of tragedy: given Ralegh as he was, given the men who formed his society, and the times in which he found himself, the conclusion was inescapable. With solemn flatness, David Lloyd remarked that Ralegh 'was one so tossed by Fortune that he was sometimes high, sometimes low, sometimes in a middle condition'— like the Grand Old Duke of York. We need a word of richer meaning than Fortune to account for the vicissitudes in Ralegh's life.

If we can be impressed by the magnitude of man's aspirations, Ralegh will impress us. It is surely not failure to have conceived and tried to carry out so many splendid designs, and no simple moral judgment will satisfactorily explain why the pursuit of these designs ended in despair and death. His story disturbs us with questionings and wonder; it is a new sense of the mystery of what carves out a man's destiny that remains when we contemplate the 'broken monuments of his great desires'.

SELECT BIBLIOGRAPHY

(A brief guide to further reading)

A. BIBLIOGRAPHY

T. N. Brushfield, A BIBLIOGRAPHY OF SIR WALTER RALEGH KNT. (2nd ed., revised and enlarged, 1908).

B. EDITIONS

(for editions of THE HISTORY OF THE WORLD, see Brushfield).

THE WORKS OF SIR WALTER RALEGH, KT. (2 vols., 1751) (does not include THE HISTORY OF THE WORLD).

THE WORKS OF SIR WALTER RALEGH, KT. (8 vols., 1829).

THE POEMS OF SIR WALTER RALEGH, edited by A. M. C. Latham; (a) (1929), (b) The Muses' Library (1951).

THE DISCOVERIE OF THE LARGE AND BEWTIFUL EMPIRE OF GUIANA, edited by V. T. Harlow (1928).

SIR WALTER RALEIGH : SELECTIONS FROM HIS 'HISTORIE OF THE WORLD', HIS LETTERS ETC., edited by G. E. Hadow (1917).

C. BIOGRAPHY

Sir Robert Naunton, FRAGMENTA REGALIA (1641), edited by E. Arber, ENGLISH REPRINTS (1870).

John Aubrey, BRIEF LIVES, edited by Andrew Clark (2 vols., 1898). An unexpurgated text of the life of Ralegh is given in the edition by Oliver Lawson Dick (1949).

N

William Oldys, THE LIFE OF SIR WALTER RALEGH, prefixed to THE HISTORY OF THE WORLD (1736), reprinted in WORKS (1829).

Edward Edwards, THE LIFE OF SIR WALTER RALEGH . . . TOGETHER WITH HIS LETTERS (2 vols., 1868).

William Stebbing, SIR WALTER RALEGH (1891); reissued with corrections (1899).

V. T. Harlow, RALEGH'S LAST VOYAGE (1932).

Edward Thompson, SIR WALTER RALEGH (1935).

D. B. Quinn, RALEIGH AND THE BRITISH EMPIRE (Teach Yourself History Library) (1947).

A. M. C. Latham, 'Sir Walter Ralegh's Gold Mine: New Light on the last Guiana Voyage', ESSAYS AND STUDIES (The English Association), (1951).

D. THE RENAISSANCE IMAGINATION

Ernest A. Strathmann, SIR WALTER RALEGH, A STUDY IN ELIZABETHAN SKEPTICISM (1951). (Important special studies on this subject by Professor Strathmann preceded this book; the references are given in his notes.)

R. W. Battenhouse, MARLOWE'S TAMBURLAINE (1941) (see pp. 50–68).

G. T. Buckley, ATHEISM IN THE ENGLISH RENAISSANCE (1932).

G. B. Harrison (editor), WILLOBIE HIS AVISA (1594) (1926).

F. R. Johnson, ASTRONOMICAL THOUGHT IN RENAISSANCE ENGLAND (1937).

F. R. Johnson, 'Gresham College: Precursor of the Royal Society', JOURNAL OF THE HISTORY OF IDEAS, i (1940).

P. H. Kocher, CHRISTOPHER MARLOWE (1946).

E. G. R. Taylor, TUDOR GEOGRAPHY, 1485–1583 (1930)

and LATE TUDOR AND EARLY STUART GEOGRAPHY, 1583–1650 (1934).

I. A. Shapiro, 'The Mermaid Club', MODERN LANGUAGE REVIEW, xlv (January 1950); see also P. Simpson, *ibid.*, xlvi (January 1951).

E. POETRY AND PROSE

M. C. Bradbrook, THE SCHOOL OF NIGHT (1936).

A. M. Buchan, 'Ralegh's CYNTHIA—Facts or Legend', MODERN LANGUAGE QUARTERLY, i (1940).

C. H. Firth, 'Sir Walter Ralegh's HISTORY OF THE WORLD', ESSAYS HISTORICAL AND LITERARY (1938).

K. Koller, 'Spenser and Ralegh', ENGLISH LITERARY HISTORY, i (1934).

J. W. Saunders. 'The Stigma of Print: a Note on the Social Bases of Tudor Poetry', ESSAYS IN CRITICISM, i (April 1951).

L. Stapleton, 'Halifax and Ralegh', JOURNAL OF THE HISTORY OF IDEAS, ii (1941).

C. F. Tucker Brooke, 'Sir Walter Ralegh as Poet and Philosopher', ESSAYS ON SHAKESPEARE AND OTHER ELIZABETHANS (1948).

See also Latham under B. and Strathmann under D.

INDEX

Milton, John, 46, 67, 70, 138, 147, 174
Minos, 160
Mitcham, 138
Monopolies, 6
More, Sir Thomas, 24
Morequito, Chief, 135
Moses, 159
Moyle, Henry, 3

Naunton, Sir Robert, 1, 6, 8, 48
Newfoundland, 3
Northumberland, Henry Percy, Earl of, 9–10, 25, 31, 57, 148

Oakeshott, W. F., 48n
Oedipus, 160
Oldys, William, 13, 14, 75
Orinoco, River, 15–19, 33, 34–9
Oxford, Edward de Vere, Earl of, 52

Paget, Henry, Lord, 52
Panama, 13
Parsons, Robert, 56, 57
Pembroke, Earl of, 39
Pererius, Benedict, 149 and n
Perrot, Sir John, 169
Perrot, Sir Thomas, 3
Petrarch, 49n
Philip, King, of Spain, 41
Philip of Macedon, 168
Phoenix Nest, The, 101
Pico della Mirandola, 49n
Popham, Sir John, 29, 30, 56
Preston, Captain Amyas, 134
Prometheus, 159
Putijma, Chieftain, 19
Puttenham, George, 52, 151

Ralegh, Carew (son of Sir Walter), 31, 44
Ralegh, Carew (half-brother to Sir Walter), 64
Ralegh, George, 34
Ralegh, Katherine, 1
Ralegh, Lady (Elizabeth Throckmorton), 2, 13–14, 15, 31, 39, 138
Ralegh, Sir Walter: birth, 1; France, Oxford and Inns of Court, 1–2; sea-exploits, 3, 13, 20–3; in Ire-

land, 3–5, 12–13; the Queen's favourite, 5–7; appointments and offices, 7; the Great Carrack, 8; colonial endeavours, 55; — in N. America, 10–12; — in Ireland, 12–13; marriage, 13–14; in Parliament, 7, 14, 24–5; expeditions to Guiana, 15–20, 32–9, 134–8, 170–1; at Cadiz, 20–22, 131–3; Islands Voyage, 22–3; attitude to succession, 25–6; dismissed by James, 26; arrest and trial, 27–31; in the Tower, 31–2; plans to obtain gold, 32; released, 32; preparations for Guiana, 33–4; return from last expedition, 39–42; attempted flight, 42–3; execution, 44–5

Ambition, 54–5, 172; arrogance, 8–10; learning, 48–50, 147–50, 156–7; luxuries, 9; medical work, 31, 61; moral values, 4, 13, 25, 141–3, 172–3; policy towards Ireland, 4–5;—towards Spain, 20, 26, 54, 131, 140; popularity, 8, 10, 25; religion, 56–8, 61–71, 153–7; science, 31, 58–61; shipbuilding, 60–1; versatility, 47–54

Poetry, 2, 53–4, 72–126, 173–174; lyrics, 51, 72–5, 81–96, 100–1; *Ocean to Cynthia,* 14, 53, 72–3, 76, 77, 78, 80, 83, 84, 87, 88, 96–124; diction, 76–7; function of poetry, 52, 79, 107; imagery, 72, 80, 110–11, 114–15; repetitions, 72–4; rhetoric, 77–80; 'sincerity', 87–90, 107–10

Prose works: *Apology,* 36, 42, 44, 137–8; *Cabinet Council,* 138; *Cause of War,* 133, 144–6; *Discovery of Guiana,* 19–20, 60, 128, 134–7; *History of World,* 31, 49, 51, 54, 55, 58, 60, 63, 66–70, 73, 133, 139, 144, 174, 175; composition, 146–50; purpose, 150–154; philosophy of, 154–7; chronology, 157–9; treatment of myths, 159–60; style, 167–70; *Instructions to Son,* 4–5, 73, 141–4, 146; *Maxims of State,* 138, 146;